D0884500

Let's
Know the
BIBLE

Let's Know the BIBLE

John W. Cawood

Fleming H. Revell Company

Old Tappan, New Jersey

Scripture quotations in this volume are from the *King James Version of the Bible* unless otherwise identified.

Scripture quotations identified ASV are from the *American Standard Version of the Revised Bible,* copyrighted 1946 by the International Council of Religious Education, and used by permission.

SBN 8007-0431-2

*To those two groups
that have challenged me to study the Word,
my teachers and my students.*

Contents

		Page
1	THE STORY	11
	The Old Testament—Preparation for the Redeemer	12
	The New Testament—	
	The Appearance of the Redeemer	14
	The New Testament—The Spreading of the Gospel	17
2	THE STRUCTURE OF THE BIBLE	20
	A General Look at the Bible	21
	An Historical Look at the Bible	24
	The Complete Picture	37
3	WHERE AND WHEN	42
	Geography	42
	Chronology	47
4	HISTORICAL BOOKS	50
	Pentateuch (Genesis through Deuteronomy)	50
	Joshua through 2 Samuel	58
	1 Kings through Esther	65
5	POETICAL BOOKS	76
	Job	76

Psalms 78
Proverbs 80
Ecclesiastes 82
Song of Solomon 84

6 PROPHETIC BOOKS 87

Major Prophets 87
Pre-Exilic Minor Prophets 96
Post-Exilic Minor Prophets 108

7 NEW TESTAMENT HISTORY 111

Matthew 111
Mark 113
Luke 114
John 116
Acts 118

8 PAUL'S EPISTLES 121

Romans through Galatians 121
Ephesians through 2 Thessalonians 127
1 Timothy through Hebrews 134

9 GENERAL EPISTLES AND THE REVELATION 141

James through 2 Peter 141
1 John through Jude 145
The Revelation 148

10 CONCLUSION 151

Appendixes: CHART AND MAPS 153

Let's Know the BIBLE

1
The Story

The Bible is indeed a wonderful book. It is a book that children can enjoy, and it is a book that learned men can read with real stimulation. But for all its wonderfulness, it is still a much misunderstood book. The average reader of the Bible does not really know the story that the Word of God is telling. And it is telling a story.

The average church member finds himself in much the same spot as the unsaved man when it comes to understanding the things in the Bible. To be sure, "the natural man receiveth not the things of the Spirit of God" (1 Corinthians 2:14), but often the saved man is in the same situation. When the church member is asked to summarize the Bible story, he is at a loss in many instances. The story or message of the Bible becomes a meaningless set of sentences that have no real movement.

Perhaps the answer given most frequently is that the Bible speaks about Christ. According to most statements He is to be seen on every page. To be sure, Christ *is* the theme of the Bible; but this does not really tell the story. The main problem is to see how the Bible story is told so that the message of Christ and the redemption He offers is clearly understood.

The Bible story can be summarized into three main ideas and movements. The Old Testament is the story of the nation of Israel as a preparation for the coming of God's Son. The New Testament then can be divided into two sections that round out the message. Christ Himself is the theme of one of these sections and the Church becomes the central idea in the last movement. These three divisions of the story of the Bible

11

will be seen in more detail so that the reader of the Bible may feel more at home in the book.

The Old Testament—Preparation for the Redeemer

In a real way the Old Testament can be summed up in a few words. The story of the Jewish nation is in reality a simple one. There are some very profound implications of the progress and continuance of this nation, but the story itself can be told in simple words. This can be seen in a graphic manner by noting that Stephen told the summary of Old Testament history in such short, yet detailed, fashion that the writer of Acts could write it in less than one chapter (Acts 7). The same conclusion can be reached by reading Nehemiah 9, the confession of the Levites and priests.

The story of Israel must begin with the Garden of Eden. God promised a redeemer immediately upon the sin of our first parents when He told Adam and Eve that the seed of the woman would crush the head of the serpent (Genesis 3:15). It is this promise that brings the nation of Israel to the place of being the manner in which God brings this redeemer.

Abraham becomes the focal point of the history of the nation of Israel, for it is he who is the father of this chosen people. The words of Stephen are clear to this point:

> . . . The God of glory appeared unto our father Abraham, when he was in Mesopotamia, before he dwelt in Charran, And said unto him, Get thee out of thy country, and from thy kindred, and come into the land which I shall shew thee. Then came he out of the land of the Chaldaeans, and dwelt in Charran: and from thence, when his father was dead, he removed him into this land, wherein ye now dwell (Acts 7:2–4).

Thus the nation of Israel had its beginning in the land of the Chaldaeans with the man Abraham.

It is in the land of Palestine that Abraham is blessed by God, and soon this one man becomes the father of the nation of Israel. Isaac was the son of promise born to Abraham and

Sarah, and then two sons were born to Isaac and Rebecca. One of these sons, Esau, became the father of the Edomite nation, while the other son, Jacob, became the father of the twelve tribes which make up the nation of Israel. With the birth and development of the sons of Jacob, the nation of Israel starts to take on new meaning and movement. Now in reality the nation as a nation starts to exist.

The land of Egypt becomes the next important chapter in the story of the nation. It is this land that harbors the family of Jacob for a time until this small family becomes in truth a large group of people. When Jacob went to Egypt, his family numbered seventy-five; when the nation came out of Egypt there were six hundred thousand men able to go to war. Listen again to the sermon of Stephen:

And he gave him the covenant of circumcision: and so Abraham begat Isaac, and circumcised him the eighth day; and Isaac begat Jacob; and Jacob begat the twelve patriarchs. . . . Then sent Joseph, and called his father Jacob to him, and all his kindred, threescore and fifteen souls (Acts 7:8, 14).

Moses is perhaps one of the most familiar characters of the Bible. Most will remember that it is this man who leads the nation of Israel out of Egypt and almost into the land of Palestine. God worked in marvelous ways with the nation to get them out of Egypt and then to care for them while they wandered in the wilderness until the time appointed for them to enter the land that had been promised to them.

He brought them out, after that he had shewed wonders and signs in the land of Egypt, and in the Red sea, and in the wilderness forty years (Acts 7:36).

Under Joshua the people of Israel enter the land of Palestine and conquer the people. Now the nation is a large group of people, and they have a land. For the next four hundred years this baby nation starts to grow and to experience what might be called growth pains. The time from Joshua to the first king of Israel, Saul, is not a time of achievement for the nation. In fact, Stephen skips this phase of Israel's history altogether.

With Saul a new feature of the story begins. This is the aspect of the kings of Israel. The nation of Israel had many kings in this period of their history. Saul, David, and Solomon were the first three of these kings; and by the time these three have ruled, the nation is one of the most respected and perhaps feared nations of the world.

After King Solomon the nation of Israel divided into two kingdoms. The story is involved at this point, but it can be summed up by saying that both kingdoms departed from Jehovah and as a consequence God caused both of them to be taken into captivity. The northern kingdom was taken away by the nation of Assyria, and the southern kingdom was captured by the Babylonians.

After the captivity of the nation of Israel, the story of the Old Testament fast draws to a close with the return of some of the captives from Babylon under Zerubbabel, Ezra, and Nehemiah. The Old Testament concludes with the nation again back in the land of Palestine, with the city of Jerusalem rebuilt and the temple again in use.

Thus one can think his way through the history of the nation of Israel in the Old Testament and in so doing think his way through the Old Testament. The story in a nutshell is: A promise of a redeemer is given; then the nation that will bring forth this redeemer is started by calling one man and blessing him so that a nation issues from him. This nation is then established in the land of Palestine, where the redeemer is to be born and a kingdom is established that is a small prototype of the Kingdom of God's Son. This nation goes into captivity because of its sins and then, because of God's faithfulness, finds itself back in the land awaiting the birth of the king and the redeemer.

The New Testament—The Appearance of the Redeemer

The story of the Christ as recorded in the New Testament is very much like the story of Israel. Though very profound and dynamic in every aspect, it may be summed up in a few words. Also, it is interesting that the main ideas or movements in Israel's history find a parallel in the life of Jesus.

On at least three separate occasions the Word of God records a very brief history of Christ. Two of these are by Peter and the third is by Paul.

> Ye men of Israel, hear these words; Jesus of Nazareth, a man approved of God among you by miracles and wonders and signs, which God did by him in the midst of you, as ye yourselves also know: Him, being delivered by the determinate counsel and foreknowledge of God, ye have taken, and by wicked hands have crucified and slain: Whom God hath raised up . . . (Acts 2:22–24).

> That word, I say, ye know, which was published throughout all Judaea, and began from Galilee, after the baptism which John preached; How God anointed Jesus of Nazareth with the Holy Ghost and with power: who went about doing good, and healing all that were oppressed of the devil; for God was with him. And we are witnesses of all things which he did both in the land of the Jews, and in Jerusalem; whom they slew and hanged on a tree: Him God raised up the third day, and shewed him openly (Acts 10:37–40).

> Of this man's seed hath God according to his promise raised unto Israel a Saviour, Jesus: when John had first preached before his coming the baptism of repentance to all the people of Israel. . . . For they that dwell at Jerusalem, and their rulers, because they knew him not. . . . And though they found no cause of death in him, yet desired they Pilate that he should be slain. And when they had fulfilled all that was written of him, they took him down from the tree, and laid him in a sepulchre. But God raised him from the dead (Acts 13:23–30).

Thus it may be seen that the life of Jesus can be recorded in one paragraph, and yet many volumes could also be written about the life of this Man.

The story of the life of Christ begins with the promise given to the parents of John the Baptizer, and then the promise given to Mary, that the redeemer was to be born. After the birth of John, Mary and Joseph are called to leave their home and go to another city. It is while in this city that Mary brought forth her firstborn and laid Him in a manger. This part of the story is perhaps the best known part, for this is the Christmas story.

Just as the nation of Israel went to Egypt for its formative years, so Jesus was taken to Egypt for his early days. After there was a change in the king of Judea, the family of Jesus returned to Palestine and took up residence in Nazareth. Here Jesus grew into the Man who was soon to die for the sins of the world.

Of the first thirty years of Jesus' life we know very little. We know he was born, and we know much of the circumstances surrounding His birth. We know He went to Egypt, but of what the family did there we know nothing. We know He grew up in Nazareth and went to Jerusalem with His parents when He was twelve, but we really do not know anything else about this phase of His life.

It is of the three-and-one-half years of His life before His death that we know the most. His life was composed of going about doing good, as Peter said. He appointed twelve men to be with Him and to preach with Him, and these men we know as His twelve apostles. Truly miracles of great significance and measure were performed by Him in these years. His preaching was heralded by friend and foe alike as being different from any that had been heard.

And then came the time for Him to die. This was the reason He came into the world. The sin of the world had to be placed on the Lamb of God. In God's plan Christ died at the hands of wicked men; but more than that, He was being judged by God the Father for men's sins. This, too, is perhaps a known part of His life since must people know something about the Easter story. At least the main facts are known by many, although most do not comprehend the significance of these events.

Again, just like the nation of Israel, Christ returns to the land, for He was raised from the dead. Israel came back to Palestine from her captivity and Christ returned after three days and three nights in the tomb. Jesus returned to finish making preparation of the disciples for their ministry in the Church.

The New Testament is the story of the Redeemer. He appeared in the town of Bethlehem, born to the virgin Mary, and He lived in Palestine for the better part of His short life. After a short ministry, He gave His life as ransom for the people of the world. On the eventful Sunday when the women went to the tomb, they found it empty, and Christ the Redeemer was alive again and forevermore. This, in brief, is the story of the New Testament as it bears on the appearance of Jesus Christ the Redeemer.

The New Testament—The Spreading of the Gospel

The disciples were commissioned to spread the message of the death and resurrection of the Redeemer to all the world. The story of the rest of the New Testament is the story of how this message of good news was spread to the disciples' world.

The story of Israel began with a birth, as did the story of Christ. This last part of the Bible message likewise can be said to begin with a birth. On the day of Pentecost, just a short time after the death and resurrection of Jesus, a new program was started. The Church, the Body of Jesus Christ, was born on this day of history. It is this new group that becomes the instrument of God to continue the story of Jesus the Redeemer. The nation of Israel was the instrument that God used to get His Son into the world, and the Church is the instrument that God uses to get the message of His Son into the world.

On the birthday of the Church we can see a preview of the purpose and dynamic of the Church. After Peter preached his sermon that centered in Jesus Christ, there were three thousand people that responded. Thus we see the Church impowered by the Spirit, preaching the good news of salvation in Christ, and people from every walk and geography responding.

The first phase of the spread of the Gospel centers in the

work of the man Peter and in the work of those associated with him. To Peter was given the privilege of first spreading the news. Throughout the land of Palestine Peter and the disciples went with the message and throughout the land people responded to this preaching.

One of those that responded was the man Paul. Paul had been a Jew who thought of the message of Christ as a direct heresy against God. But he soon found that Jesus was God in flesh who died for man. With the conversion of Paul to this new way, the story of the New Testament takes on another turn.

Peter went throughout the land of Palestine with the news, while Paul spent most of his time spreading the message to people and lands where others had not gone. With Paul the Gospel went to Asia Minor, to Macedonia, to Greece, and then on to Rome and perhaps even on to Spain. It is the story of Paul's journeys and his establishment of churches that occupies the bulk of the remaining part of the New Testament.

When we finally get the Gospel to Rome, and when we finally come to the end of Paul's life, we are, for the most part, through with the story of the Bible. Very little is told of Peter's later life and nothing is really known or told in the Bible of the other disciples except that John is seen after many years on the Isle of Patmos in exile because of the testimony of Christ. The Old Testament story ended with Israel in the land awaiting the coming of the Redeemer. The first part of the New Testament story ended with the Redeemer teaching the disciples for the coming ministry. The last part of the New Testament story ends with the disciple (i.e., John, Revelation 22) looking for the coming again of the Redeemer for His own and to the world.

Summary

The story of the Bible is indeed a simple, yet very profound, one. The reader of the Bible needs to know that the Bible is telling a story, and it can be put together and thought through.

As one can think about the nation of Israel and its beginning, its formation, its kings, its captivities, and its return, then the Old Testament becomes a book with a real message. As one can think through the life of Jesus in His birth, travels, preachings, miracles, death, and resurrection, then the first part of the New Testament becomes likewise alive and meaningful. The New Testament story then is complete with an understanding of the spread of the message of Christ as seen in the life of Peter and then in the life of Paul.

The theme of the Bible *is* Jesus Christ, and no one will understand the Bible until he sees Him. But to see the movement and true story of the Bible as seen in Christ, one must also see the complete story of Israel as a nation as preparation for the coming of Christ and, also, the story of the Church as the means of spreading the news of the coming(s) of Christ.

2

The Structure
of the Bible

It is important that the story or message of the Bible be understood before one can feel at home in this book. It is always the case that unfamiliar ground leads to misunderstanding, and this is very true in the realm of the Bible. The more a reader feels comfortable in his knowledge of what the Bible is talking about, the more he can understand as he continues to read and study.

Once a reader has somewhat mastered the gist of the Bible, he needs to go on in his understanding of the Bible as a whole by properly relating each of the books of the Bible to the story of the Bible. Each book fits into the complete picture, and we need to know where.

In order to better acquaint the reader with the books of the Bible in their relation to the story of the Bible, it will be necessary to look at the structure of the Bible. Just as a carpenter needs to be familiar with each one of his tools and what each is for, so the reader of the Word of God needs to be familiar with the parts of the Bible and how they are to be used in the overall picture.

This chapter will cover three main areas. First, the general view of the Bible will be presented so that all the books of the Bible can be seen and recognized as a part of the whole. Then the historical story will be retold in such a way as to make each book that shares this story to be clearly seen in its relation to the others and the connected history of Israel, Christ, and the Church. Finally, it will be necessary for the books that are not directly historical to be related to this historical presentation. The reader will then be able to place each book in its proper place in an overall picture, and in so doing will feel much more at home in the Bible. We need ever to remember that the Bible was written out of an historical context, and it is only as we recognize this context that we will be able to understand the message that God has for us.

A General Look at the Bible

The Bible is one book that can be divided in various ways. This one book is made up of sixty-six books that go together to make the whole. Many readers of the Bible do not feel at home simply because they do not know what books are really in the Bible. Many a Sunday school student has been fooled in a "sword drill" (looking up references in the Bible) when the leader has asked the students to turn to Hezekiah 1:1 (there is no such book). Also, many a church member has spent most of the Sunday morning service trying to find a book like Obadiah or Jude (they are so small that if two pages are stuck together you will lose them).

The index or table of contents that is in the front of every Bible is a very nice thing to know or to be familiar with. Just to know what books are in the Bible and where they occur is worthwhile knowledge.

The books as they appear in our English Bible of today are:

Genesis	2 Chronicles	Daniel
Exodus	Ezra	Hosea
Leviticus	Nehemiah	Joel
Numbers	Esther	Amos
Deuteronomy	Job	Obadiah
Joshua	Psalms	Jonah
Judges	Proverbs	Micah
Ruth	Ecclesiastes	Nahum
1 Samuel	Song of Solomon	Habakkuk
2 Samuel	Isaiah	Zephaniah
1 Kings	Jeremiah	Haggai

| 2 Kings | Lamentations | Zechariah |
| 1 Chronicles | Ezekiel | Malachi |

Matthew	Ephesians	Hebrews
Mark	Philippians	James
Luke	Colossians	1 Peter
John	1 Thessalonians	2 Peter
Acts	2 Thessalonians	1 John
Romans	1 Timothy	2 John
1 Corinthians	2 Timothy	3 John
2 Corinthians	Titus	Jude
Galatians	Philemon	Revelation

This is the list of books, and this is the order in which they appear. It is heartily recommended that every reader of the Bible who wants to understand the book commit this list to memory.

There are thirty-nine books in the Old Testament and there are twenty-seven books in the New Testament. These books may be grouped in smaller numbers; by so doing their basic content can be better understood and their place in the story can start to be seen.

The Jews early divided the Old Testament into three divisions. These divisions and the books that are found in each are:

The Law
> Genesis, Exodus, Leviticus, Numbers, Deuteronomy

The Prophets
> Former Prophets
>> Joshua, Judges, Samuel (all one book),
>> Kings (all one book)
> Latter Prophets
>> Major
>>> Isaiah, Jeremiah, Ezekiel
>> Minor (all one book)
>>> Hosea, Joel, Amos, Obadiah, Jonah, Micah, Nahum, Habakkuk, Zephaniah, Haggai, Zechariah, Malachi

The Writings
    Poetical
        Psalms, Proverbs, Job
    Rolls
        Song of Solomon, Ruth, Lamentations, Ecclesiastes, Esther
    Historical
        Daniel, Ezra-Nehemiah (one book), Chronicles (one book)

It will be noted that this list contains all the books as they are in our English Bible, but they are in some cases joined together so that there are only twenty-four books instead of the thirty-nine that we have; yet all the books are there.

In the Septuagint (a Greek translation of the Old Testament made about 250 B.C.) and in the Vulgate (a Latin translation of the Bible made about A.D. 390) there is the division of the books of the Old Testament into the present thirty-nine books rather than the twenty-four.

By basically following the Jewish division or groups of the books of the Old Testament, most students of the Bible divided these books into four or five simple divisions.

The Law
    Genesis through Deuteronomy

Historical
    Joshua through Esther

Poetical
    Job through Song of Solomon

Major Prophets
    Isaiah through Daniel

Minor Prophets
    Hosea through Malachi

This grouping of the books allows the reader to know at a glance where he is (in general) in the story. The Law section is related to the beginning of the nation of Israel. The Historical section actually completes the rest of the story of Israel as it is found in the Old Testament. The Poets and the Prophets fit back into the above two section as commentary on the happenings of the periods.

The New Testament can also be grouped so that the reader knows in general where he is in the story. A common division is:

Gospels—the story of Christ's life
    Matthew, Mark, Luke, John

Acts—the story of the Church

Paul's Epistles
    Romans through Philemon
        (some would say Hebrews)

General Epistles
    James through Jude

Revelation—the climax of the story

The Gospels and the Book of Acts tell the story of the New Testament, and the rest of the books either fit into the Book of Acts or are between the end of Acts and the writing of the Book of the Revelation.

This, in general, is the Bible. Each book is related to the whole picture and to a part of the picture. As the reader of the Bible becomes more familiar with this general view, he will be able to comprehend the parts more easily.

An Historical Look at the Bible

The student of the Bible needs to distinguish between the books that are involved with the actual history being told and the books that are complementary to those books. The student also needs to know how the books that are telling the story fit together in a complete picture.

To facilitate that understanding of this important area, it seems best to make some sort of a chart that can be followed. The chart on page 155 has been made to help in putting the books of the Bible into a meaningful picture for the reader.

To begin with, it may be seen that only the books that move the story along are to be found in this chart. These books are simply Genesis through Nehemiah and Matthew through Acts. The rest of the books of the Bible can be made to fit into the picture painted by these books. Let's look at the chart and the story in more detail.

Formation   Genesis begins the story just as it begins the Bible. The story of Genesis is the story of beginnings. It is the story of the formation of all things and, in particular, it is the story of the formation of the nation of Israel.

The Book of Genesis begins in the dateless past when God created the world. This begins the drama of redemption. With the creation of the world and man we are immediately shown the need for bringing man into a relation with the Creator.

The book begins in the Garden of Eden with God and man in fellowship. Soon we find that man has disobeyed God and has plunged mankind into the desperate place of need that man finds himself in today. The writer of Genesis takes us on in history through the genealogy of Adam to show how man spread throughout the world and to show that he is very much in need of help from God.

On through the flood with its almost complete annihilation of man from the face of the earth, Moses continues his story. The focal point of the book is soon reached, for by the time the reader has reached the twelfth chapter, he finds himself face to face with Abraham, the father of the nation of Israel.

The message of Genesis continues by showing how Isaac was born to Abraham and Sarah and then by showing how Isaac obtained his wife, with Esau and Jacob being born to this union. Half of the Book of Genesis is devoted to showing the development of the Jewish nation through Isaac and Jacob.

As we come to the end of the book we find that to Jacob has been born twelve sons that are now the body of people through whom God will continue the story and preparation for the redeemer. Jacob and his sons are brought to Egypt by the providence of God, and there the family becomes a mighty people.

Thus, this first book in the Bible (and in the chart) begins with the creation of man and ends with the nation of Israel formed and in the land of Egypt.

Deliverance   As the family of Jacob grew more and more into a large people, and as, with the passing of time, kings came to the throne in Egypt that did not know the history of this people, so more and more frequently they were subjected to bondage in this land that had harbored them. The Book of Exodus moves the reader on in this fascinating story of Israel showing how God delivers them from the hand of the Egyptians.

The Book of Exodus begins with the birth of Moses. The story of Moses' birth and adoption by the Pharaoh of Egypt is indeed a thrilling one. God is preparing Moses to be His deliverer by having him trained in the vast knowledge of the Egyptians and in all the skills that it will take to bring this mighty people out of Egypt and into the land that is rightly theirs by the promise of God to Abraham, Isaac, and Jacob.

Moses soon entered into the plight of his people by delivering a Jew from an Egyptian, only to find that his people did not recognize him as God's deliverer. So Moses fled to the desert to be further trained by God. Upon his return forty years later under the direction and preparation of God, he was able to captain the Jewish people and bring them out of their bondage.

Almost half of the Book of Exodus is concerned with the raising up on Moses, the contest with the Pharaoh of Egypt to let Israel go, and with the actual leaving (the Exodus) of Egypt bound for the land of promise. The rest of the book is involved with the giving of the Law from Mount Sinai and with the giving of the instructions for the making of the Tabernacle, as well as with the actual making of this building that was the center of worship for the nation of Israel for the next four hundred years.

Wanderings   The Book of Numbers is the next book that is involved with moving the history along. This book begins with the people at Mount Sinai and takes them to the eastern border of the promised land.

26

The book gets its name from the fact that twice in this book people are numbered. Once in the first part of the book and once in the latter part of the book a census is taken to determine the number of fighting men in the nation of Israel (see chapter 1 and chapter 26).

A better title, as far as understanding the contents of the book is concerned, might be the Book of Wanderings. In this book we find God leading the nation of Israel from Sinai to a spot in the south of the Promised Land. From this spot (Kadesh-barnea) spies were sent out to look at the land and to tell the people about it. And at this spot the people of Israel rebelled against God and voted not to go into the land because of the giants. As a consequence of this rebellion, God made the nation to wander in the wilderness for the next thirty-eight years until all the people that were over twenty years of age at the time of the decision had died.

When the last of the rebel people had died, then God was ready to lead the nation into the land of Palestine. The last few chapters of the Book of Numbers relate the final stages of this journey and take the people of Israel right up to the borders of the land on the east side of the River Jordan.

Conquering   The fourth book in the historical sequence is the Book of Joshua. This book very graphically describes how the nation of Israel fought for and gained control of the land of Palestine.

It has often been suggested that if Israel had entered the land when God offered it to them while they were at Kadesh-barnea, they would not have had to fight for it; but God would have in some way made it possible for them to possess the land without "firing a shot." Because of their disobedience they had to fight for possession of the land that God had promised to *give* to them.

The Book of Joshua begins with the nation on the east side of Jordan (where Numbers had left them) and then proceeds to get them into the land. It is at this point in the story that Moses is replaced by Joshua. Moses, too, had not obeyed God and Joshua had been appointed to take his place when Moses died. The first task of Joshua was to lead the nation across the River Jordan and on into the fight for the land.

Such cities as Jericho and Ai became the first battles that the nation must fight. Then on through the land, in which has been called the northern and southern campaigns, Joshua leads the people in the battle for the land of Palestine. Finally, the inhabitants of the land are subjected to the government of the nation of Israel and the nation now has a land.

The land must be divided or allotted to the various parts of the nation, and this work is described in the other chapters of the book. By the end of this book we find the nation settling down in their new land and beginning to adjust to the requirements and regulations that God has for them.

Declension   Perhaps one of the darkest periods in the history of the nation of Israel is the period known as the period of the Judges. During this period the nation departed from following God so often that it becomes a routine in the Book of Judges.

The nation of Israel had failed to drive out all of the inhabitants of the land and had started to mingle with them as the Book of Joshua closed. The Book of Judges starts at this point and shows the dire results of such action. The people that Israel tried to live with soon became her masters, and Israel found herself a captive in her own land.

As the nation would repent of their folly and cry unto God, there would be a deliverer raised up. Such men as Othniel, Jehud, Gideon, Jephthah, Samson, and even a woman named Deborah, were brought to a place of delivering the nation from their foes. These deliverers were also called judges, and it is from these that the book and the period get their name.

Judges ends with a very dismal picture. Religious indifference, moral decay, and governmental laxity are all found as results of the nation playing with sin. Truly, this is a dark picture which is painted in this portion of the Word of God.

Saul   Technically, the last of the judges was Samuel. This man is perhaps one of the most God-centered judges that the nation had. But it is in the period that Samuel judged Israel that the nation asked for a king, and thus begins a very important phase of the history of the nation.

The first king of the nation of Israel was Saul. Israel had seen that the nations around them had men to lead in war and men to lead in the affairs of state; they decided that this would be good for them. God picked their first king according to what He knew they wanted. Saul was a fine specimen of a man, one that was not afraid to fight. When the people knew Saul had been picked to be their king, they were most pleased.

The Book of 1 Samuel gives us not only the history of Israel under the judgeship of Samuel, but it gives to us the complete story of the man Saul and his reign. As the reign of Saul unfolds, it soon becomes apparent that he is not a man that can lead the people in the ways of God. On a number of occasions he shows that he does not plan to be God's man. Thus, also in this book God has recorded for us the choosing of the second king for the nation of Israel. This man who is to succeed Saul is another of the famous men of the Bible. The man's name is David.

After presenting Samuel and Saul, the Book of 1 Samuel continues the history of Israel by showing how Saul sought to kill David and how David was forced to flee for his life. The book ends with David in hiding and with Saul dead.

David   The entire Book of 2 Samuel is devoted to the life of the man David. David, like Saul, reigned for a period of forty years, and these years are described in this book.

David was a man after God's own heart, and this period was one of Israel's best; but the man and the period were not without trouble. David's troubles began immediately for the nation of Israel divided over his being king. Some put forth one of the sons of Saul as king and only a few tribes recognized David as their king.

Soon, however, David was recognized by all the twelve tribes that made up the nation and with this event the Jewish people became a real power in the world scene.

It was David who established Jerusalem as the capital of

the nation, and it was David that fought the enemies of Israel until there was peace in the land. The nation was solidified and the borders of the nation were firmly established in the time David was on the throne.

Second Samuel does not overlook David's faults. It is in this book that David's great sins are laid bare for all to see. The sins of lust, deceit, murder, adultery are all forcibly placed at David's feet. As a result of these, David experienced much of the same in his own family and life. One of his daughters was raped by one of his sons; one of his sons murdered another of his sons; one of his sons connived to displace his father in the eyes and heart of the people; and David had his heart broken many times as a result of his breaking of God's heart.

Division   The Book of 1 Kings, although it begins by presenting the spectacular reign of Solomon, brings the reader to the time in Israel's history when the nation became divided. Thus, this book and this period can best be titled by that fact.

To be sure, Solomon was a fantastic man. His rule over Israel produced such feats as to cause nations far and wide to seek his favor. And still today, when men talk of grandeur, they talk in terms of Solomon's rule over this nation, the nation that was to be God's instrument in bringing His Son into the world. His temple, his house, his wisdom, his revenue, all play a part in this book and in this part of the story of Israel.

Although Solomon had a choice father, David, and although he had a good beginning in his kingdom, he soon left a pure worship of Jehovah, and sin always brings its results. God told Solomon that He would divide the kingdom because of the folly and sin into which this king had led the nation. And so upon the death of Solomon this great nation found itself divided.

Ten of the tribes separated and established a kingdom in the northern part of Palestine. This kingdom was known as Israel, or Ephraim, and had their capital in Samaria. The remaining two tribes, Judah and Benjamin, made up the southern kingdom, and they maintained the city of Jerusalem as their capital. This division was known as Judah.

In 1 Kings, therefore, one reads of Solomon's reign and of the first fifty years of the divided kingdom. The prophet Elijah, a major character of this period of Israel's history, is also portrayed in the latter part of the book.

Captivity   The Book of 2 Kings is the ninth book of our chart and continues the story up to the time of the taking away of each kingdom into captivity.

The northern and southern kingdoms warred and jockeyed for power for a number of years. For a little over two hundred years these nations existed and fought with one another and with the people around them. These battles and the various kings that ruled in each kingdom form the content of this book. It is from the fact that there are so many kings listed in this book as well as the one previous that these books get their name. Remember that in the Hebrew Bible, these two books are one.

It would be well for the student of the Bible to be familiar with the names of the kings of each part of the division. There were nineteen kings in each of the kingdoms, with the southern kingdom having the "distinction" of one woman added to the list as a queen. The names are:

Israel	*Judah*
Jeroboam I	Rehoboam
Nadab	Abijah
Baasha	Asa
Elah	Jehosaphat
Zimri	Jehoram
Omri	Ahaziah
Ahab	Athaliah
Ahaziah	Joash
Joram	Amaziah
Jehu	Uzziah
Jehoahaz	Jotham
Joash	Ahaz
Jeroboam II	Hezekiah
Zechariah	Manasseh
Shallum	Amon

Menahem	Josiah
Pekahiah	Jehoahaz
Pekah	Jehoiakim
Hoshea	Jehoiakin
	Zedekiah

In the year 722 B.C. (two hundred plus years after the division), the northern kingdom was taken captive by the nation of Assyria. God caused this portion of the nation of Israel to be taken off the land and to serve other people because of their sin. This captivity is recorded in chapter 17 of 2 Kings.

After the northern tribes were taken way, the southern tribes remained in the land for another one hundred years. Finally, Nebuchadnezzar, as general of the Babylonian armies, came and conquered this part of the nation. Between the years 606 and 586 B.C., the Babylonian armies besieged and conquered this people. Finally, with the deportation of the people to Babylon in 586, the city of Jerusalem was burned and the great nation of Israel was now completely under the hand of foreign people.

Exile   Israel had been warned in the Book of Deuteronomy, before they ever entered the land, that God would punish them by taking them out of the land. He had warned them that they would be exiled from the land that was theirs. It is this period in Israel's history that does not have much written record.

The Book of Daniel is perhaps the main book of this period. Daniel was living in the court of Babylon during the period of the captivity of the southern tribes, and his experiences are the subject matter of his book.

What was happening in the land of Assyria with the northern tribes and much of what was happening in Babylon with the southern tribes is not known. God did not have these details recorded for us. Daniel sheds what little light can be seen on this period although most of his book has to do with the nation of Israel future to his time.

Temple   The Book of Ezra is the next real book of history that the reader finds. This book deals with the return of the people from the Babylonian captivity.

God had promised through the prophet Isaiah that a king named Cyrus would permit his people to return to their land. God had further spoken through His prophet Jeremiah that the Babylonian captivity would last for seventy years. The Book of Ezra begins with Cyrus, king of Persia, giving his decree to let those who so desired return to the land of Palestine.

Further, the Book of Ezra records for us the struggles that the people had in trying to begin again their worship of Jehovah. As they tried to build the temple, the adversaries put the pressure on them and finally on the Persian authorities to have the work stopped. With time and with the exhortation of the prophets Haggai and Zechariah, the people finished the work of building the temple and again began worshipping God there.

The City   Although the temple was rebuilt and although many of the people had rebuilt homes in the city of Jerusalem, the city itself and its walls were not being taken care of. The Book of Nehemiah continues the story of the return from exile by sharing the story of the rebuilding of the wall of the city.

As one comes to the end of the Book of Nehemiah, he is at the end of the Old Testament. The story of Israel as found in the Old Testament ends with the nation back in their land, with the temple reestablished, and with the city of Jerusalem rebuilt. The reader is again reminded that Nehemiah, chapter 9, records for us a brief history of the Old Testament. By reading this chapter and by adding the books of Ezra and Nehemiah at the end, it is possible to see the complete story of Israel—the preparation for the Redeemer.

The Silent Years   As one looks at the chart, it will be seen that the thirteenth division does not have any books associated with it. This is why the period is known as the "silent years." During the time from Nehemiah to the time of John the Baptizer, God did not speak through men. For four hundred years there is no written record of God's words.

While these years do not contain books that are worthy to

be listed in the Bible, there were books written during this time that are of interest to the Bible student. It is during this period that the books known as the Apocrypha were written. These books vary in their value to the reader of the Bible, but they are not on a par with God's Word. Even Jerome, in his Latin Vulgate, set these books apart as not being of equal value as the rest of the Old Testament. It was not until the Council of Trent in A.D. 1546 that these books were declared equal with the rest of the Bible by the Roman Catholic Church.

Also, in this period there were changes in the political scene. When the Old Testament ended, Persia was the world ruler. About seventy years later, Greece, under Alexander the Great, became the nation that ruled the world. Another one hundred and seventy years brings us to the time of the Maccabean revolt. This was a movement in the Jewish nation that attempted to break the yoke of the Greeks after that nation had greatly persecuted Israel. One hundred years later the Romans were in power, and it is this great empire that the reader of the New Testament meets.

Another important area in this period that the reader of Scripture needs to know is the area of religion in the Jewish nation. It is during this period that such institutions and groups came into being as the Sanhedrin, the synagogues, the Pharisees, the Sadducees, the Herodians, and the scribes. The reader is encouraged to study these subjects in a Bible dictionary or Bible encyclopedia.

Christ　　The story of the Redeemer is told in the first four books of the New Testament. It becomes necessary to put all these books together in order to have somewhat of a complete story of the life of Jesus Christ.

Each of the four Gospels presents a different emphasis in the life of Christ. Matthew presents Christ as the King of the Jews. Mark shows that He was here in the role of a servant. Luke magnifies the life of Christ as a man, and John writes to show the deity of the Redeemer.

As we read these four books, we can see the life of Jesus Christ unfold. No one Gospel writer, nor all four together, tell us of all the things that this One did. But enough of the story is told to make us aware of some of the vital issues in His life.

Christ was born to the virgin Mary in the town of Bethlehem in Judea. He was taken to Egypt soon after His birth to escape the wrath of King Herod the Great, and returned to Palestine after Herod's death.

The life of Jesus was lived in a city in the northern section of Palestine near the Lake of Galilee. Nazareth was the city that saw this Man grow from childhood to manhood, and watched while He learned the trade of the one that was considered his father.

The main Gospel record is a record of only three-and-one-half years of Christ's life. It is during this time that He chose His twelve disciples, performed His miracles, preached the message of the kingdom, and gave His life as ransom for the sins of the world. The story moves rather rapidly toward that eventful time when Jesus was tried and placed on a cross to die. With a great climax each of the Gospels records the resurrection of Jesus Christ and His appearances to His disciples to prove to all the world that His resurrection was real and bodily.

The Church   The Book of Acts is the only other really historical book of the New Testament. All the other books of the New Testament are either letters to churches, persons, or general messages to all.

In the Book of Acts we read of the spreading of the good news starting in Jerusalem, then on to Judea and Samaria, then on out to the lands around the Mediterranean Sea until the Apostle Paul comes to Rome with the message of the Redeemer.

This book records with clarity the acceptance of the Gospel and its Christ by common folk, and by those of the upper realms of society. It shows that the Redeemer died for and can be accepted by men, women, and children; by Jew and Gentile; by religious and irreligious; by bond and by free.

The men of this book are a study in themselves. Peter, the man who denied Christ, becomes the leader of the group and causes the message to go forward. Stephen, a waiter on tables, becomes the first martyr and example for many to follow. James, the half-brother of our Lord and an unbeliever during Christ's life, becomes the leader of the church at Jerusalem. Barnabas, a man of wealth, becomes a missionary, as do Silas and Mark. Paul, the persecuter of the Church, becomes the preacher of the same great truth. Luke, a physician, goes with Paul to evangelize the world.

The Church with its beginning on the day of Pentecost goes through many troubles with the leaders of Judaism trying to stop this work of God. Paul, however, takes the lead under the direction of God and carries the message of Christ and the truth of the Church throughout the then known world. Soon this group that started with just a handful in Jerusalem claimed sister churches in every major city and country of the area. Through persecution and peril the Church is established and the Gospel is spread.

The Completion   Although we must look to Acts for the main details of the story of the spread of the Gospel and the formation of the Church, there are some other historical facts that can be found in some of the other books of the New Testament.

From 1 and 2 Timothy and Titus we learn that Paul must have been released from prison where the Book of Acts ended and he must have traveled some more with Timothy and Titus, being left in Ephesus and Crete respectively to continue the work.

By reading 1 and 2 Peter we can see that Peter also traveled and worked with the churches. John's ministry can be somewhat pieced together by noting the three small epistles that bear his name and by noting the details of the book of Revelation.

Thus, the story ends. God has recorded for us the message and the details that He wants us to have. From the beginning of man and the beginning of the nation of Israel on through the birth and death of the Redeemer and on through the establishment of the Church the story has been told. The overall picture can be told by carefully putting twelve of the Old Testament books together in sequence and then by using the first five books of the New Testament.

The Bible makes sense. The books are there for a purpose. There is a story to be told. Learn the story and learn what part goes with which book. You will find yourself much more at home in the book you love.

The Complete Picture

Thus far we have tried to show the general structure of the Bible and also how certain books of the Bible tell the historical story that is so important to know if one is to understand the book as a whole. It is now time to fit all the books of the Bible into the picture so that the reader may know just where he is when he is reading any one book.

As the reader again looks at the chart on page 155, it becomes apparent that the story of the Bible is told in about twenty of the books. This means that there are about forty-six books that must be put into the picture to make it complete. Until each book is given its proper place in the construction of the Bible as a whole, the message of the whole or the parts will not be clear.

The chart on page 155 is an attempt to show how each book fits into the historical story. It is suggested that you keep this chart in mind as you read the following pages. Let's look at the completed picture.

Formation   The only book that might go with the Book of Genesis is the Book of Job. No other book covers the same ground or tells of events that happened in this period.

Job is often placed at a time during the patriarchs, the fathers of the Jewish nation; so the Book of Job can be placed under the Book of Genesis in the chart as belonging to this time and showing us something of the time and the people.

Deliverance   The period titled The Deliverance is the period that has the Book of Exodus as its main book. There is a book that was written at the same time, or at least the events in the book are at the same time, as the Book of Exodus; that is the Book of Leviticus.

One of the major features of the deliverance period is the stopping of the nation of Israel at Mt. Sinai and the receiving of the Law from God. From chapter 19 through the end of Exodus (chapter 40), Israel is at Sinai.

By reading such passages as Leviticus 7:38; 25:1; and 27:34, is becomes clear that this book is a further commentary on the Law and belongs to the period of the Book of Exodus.

Wanderings   Since the Book of Numbers takes the people of Israel up to the entry of the Promised Land, up to the death of Moses, there is only one book that could be in this spot—the Book of Deuteronomy.

Deuteronomy is basically a review of the events from Egypt to the borders of the land of Canaan, and also a restatement of the laws for the new generation that is about to enter the land.

The book begins with the Israelites in the plains of Moab waiting to enter, and the book ends in the same place. Thus this book should be read with the Book of Numbers in mind and with a realization that this book is not concerned with new history as much as with a review of the immediate past history. The only real new historic event of any significance is the death of Moses.

Conquering   There are no other books that belong to the period that is covered by the Book of Joshua. This is one of the few spots where the Bible has only one book to cover what is important in the time.

Declension   The Book of Judges is the darkest book of the Bible, and covers one of the darkest eras of the Jewish people. In contrast to this is the fact that God has caused to be written a book that is one of the brightest. Ruth is the book that must be read and understood in the light (or dark) of the Book of Judges. The time period of Ruth is clearly stated in 1:1 when we read, "And it came to pass in the days when the judges judged . . ." (ASV).

Saul   The Book of 1 Samuel, which relates this time to us, stands virtually alone. There is no other book to which we can go for more information or commentary. It is possible that some of the psalms of David were written in this period, but it seems best to keep the Book of Psalms for the next time period.

David   David's period is a vital period in Israel's history, and it is one of the finest as far as the leadership of the man is concerned. The importance of this period is not reflected, however, in the amount of extra writings we have for this time.

As mentioned before, it seems that some of the psalms belong to this period, since David wrote a good number of them. The only other book that covers this time period along with the Book of 2 Samuel is the Book of Chronicles.

First Chronicles is a review of the history of David with the genealogies leading up to the man. Other than these two books, this period does not have collateral material.

Division   First Kings is the book of the division, and with this book we may place three other books and part of a fourth.

Since half of 1 Kings is devoted to the reign of Solomon, we must put the books that were written by him in this section. Proverbs (for the most part), Song of Solomon, and Ecclesiastes own Solomon as their author and thus go with 1 Kings. Ten chapters of 2 Chronicles also go with 1 Kings since they contain a review of the reign of this man.

Captivity   The Book of 2 Kings is indeed a sad book. It is in this book that the nation of Israel is on the road down and two sections of the nation are carried into captivity.

It is in this day of rebellion and idolatry that God raised up the prophets to turn Israel back to Himself. Listen to God's summary of this period:

> Moreover all the chiefs of the priests, and the people, trespassed very greatly after all the abominations of the nations; and they polluted the house of Jehovah which he had hallowed in Jerusalem. And Jehovah, the God of their fathers, sent to them by his messengers, rising up early and sending, because he had compassion on his people,

and on his dwelling-place: but they mocked the messengers of God, and despised his words, and scoffed at his prophets, until the wrath of Jehovah arose against his people, till there was no remedy (2 Chronicles 36:14–16 ASV).

Thus, in this period we can expect to find most of the prophets. This section is the one that has the largest complement of books in it. Most readers of the Bible miss this fact.

The books that go in this section are: Hosea, Joel, Amos, Obadiah, Jonah, Micah, Nahum, Habakkuk, Zephaniah, Isaiah, and Jeremiah. Eleven prophets and the rest of 2 Chronicles must be understood in this context. The books that come after 2 Kings in the arrangement of our Bible do not really come after it; most come before or during the period.

Exile   With the Book of Daniel we can place the Book of Ezekiel. Both of these books deal with the time period that can be called The Exile. Part of Jeremiah and Lamentations (lamenting the fall of Jerusalem) can also be read in conjunction with this period.

Temple   In Ezra 5:1 we read, "Now the prophets Haggai the prophet, and Zechariah the son of Iddo, prophesied unto the Jews that were in Judah and Jerusalem . . ." (ASV). This shows us that the two books written by these men belong to the period of the building of the temple as it is recorded in the Book of Ezra.

The Book of Esther also must be understood and read as a book of this period. Most Bible scholars place the events of Esther between the sixth and seventh chapters of Ezra. This book gives us the background for the Jews being in favor with the Persian authorities.

The City   The last book in the Old Testament, Malachi, belongs in the last section of the history of the nation. With the books of Nehemiah and Malachi, we are brought to the end of the Old Testament part of the story that God wants us to know.

The Silent Years   As mentioned in the previous section when the history was being put together, this period does not have a book of the Bible with it. The silent years were indeed silent as to the written revelation of God.

Christ   The story of Christ as found in the four Gospels is all we have as to the life of the Redeemer. Thus there are no other books that can be placed in this section of our history.

The Church   It is during the period covered by the Book of Acts that we can place most of the books of the New Testament. From the time of the ascension of Christ to the time of Paul's imprisonment in Rome many of the New Testament epistles were written.

The Books of Romans, 1 and 2 Corinthians, Galatians, Ephesians, Philippians, Colossians, 1 and 2 Thessalonians, Philemon, Hebrews (?), James, and perhaps 1 Peter, all can be placed within the scope of the Book of Acts.

The Completion   In this last section can be placed the remainder of the books of the New Testament. Along with 1 and 2 Timothy and Titus, we can place 2 Peter, 1, 2, and 3 John, Jude, and the Revelation.

Each book of the Bible is important and has a special message for us. This message is often lost because we do not feel at home in the book, since we do not know where it fits in the story of the Bible. By putting the Bible into a meaningful order and by placing each book in its proper place, it becomes easier to see where you are in any book. Make yourself at home in the Bible by learning the story and by learning where each book fits.

41

3
Where and When

To the average student and to the average reader of the Bible there is nothing more uninteresting than a study of places and dates. Geography has caused many students to wish they were somewhere else rather than in the location they are. Yet, as we all know, we seem to get more interested in stories we hear if we have been there ourselves or know a great deal about the place where the particular story takes place. Bible geography is likewise important and will make the reader feel more at home when he can picture in his mind the movements and places being talked about.

A proper understanding of the chronology of the Bible is also meaningful and helpful. With certain dates in our understanding, we are able to place events and even books in their proper sequence. Certain books were written at certain times and these dates are important to an understanding of the contents of the books.

Geography

Palestine on a World Map   As one looks at a map of the world, one is impressed with the largeness of the continents and with the vast coverage of the seas. The Bible story is of course the most important story in the world, and one is inclined to think that such a story would be enacted on a stage of great importance and magnitude. But this is not true.

Tucked away at the east end of the Mediterranean Sea is the land known as Palestine. This small section of the world globe is the stage on which God has chosen to enact the drama of redemption. Palestine is so small it can actually be overlooked as a map of the world is viewed. The large continent of Africa lies to the south, and Europe with all its countries lies to the north. Even Arabia, which is to the southeast of Palestine, makes this land look like a meaningless strip of land.

For a full understanding of the message of the Bible and to feel completely at home in this book, I would suggest that the reader get a picture of the entire Mediterranean area. Get this picture fixed in your mind so that you know where you are at all times.

Palestine as a Land   When someone mentions Palestine, what do you think about as far as the land itself is concerned? What kind of climate do you picture? What about the topography of the land? And the actual distances between points? It is interesting how our concepts in these areas are often wrong. Not too long ago I traveled to the country of Ecuador. I was living in Florida at the time, and I thought about the possible time change since I was going to the west coast of South America. It was a real shock to look at a map (one I had looked at many times) and notice that the west coast of South America was almost directly below the east coast of North America—or, better, that I was going to go a little east to get to Ecuador.

The land of Palestine is perhaps best noted for two large bodies of water that are part of it. To the north is the Lake of Galilee, and to the south is the Dead Sea. It might be best to use these titles of each to distinguish the facts that the lake is fresh water and the sea is salt. Running between these two is the famed River Jordan. Perhaps the most surprising fact about this feature of the land is that the land between these two bodies of water is a short distance. Between Galilee and the Dead Sea there is a distance of about sixty-five miles. The Jordan is such a winding river, however, that it actually travels about two hundred miles in going from lake to sea.

The terrain of the land is also most interesting. The land is rocky and for the most part barren. There are some very fertile places in this land, but the many hills and the rocky soil make it hard for vegetation to flourish. The region around the Lake of Galilee is the most fertile and the region around the Dead Sea is the most barren.

When you read of mountains in this part of the world, you might also get the wrong impression. The highest mountain in the area (although it is really to the north of Palestine itself) is Mt. Hermon. It reaches the height of 9,232 feet. Hebron, to the south of Jerusalem, is only a little over three thousand feet. Most of the mountains that bear the name "mountain" are only three to four thousand feet in height.

This land is also marked by the fact that the two main bodies of water are both below sea level. The Lake of Galilee is 682 feet below sea level and the Dead Sea is 1286 feet below sea level. The entire Jordan Valley, therefore, is below sea level.

The climate in Palestine is really very moderate. Only in the Jordan Valley does the temperature reach the high nineties or one hundred degrees. The average temperature for the year is in the sixties, and it rarely ever gets to the freezing mark. The seasons in Palestine are not seasons in the general connatation of the word, seasons, with temperature as the main measurement. The seasons in Palestine have to do with moisture. There are only two seasons—wet and dry. From May to October is the dry season, and from November to April is the wet season. It is warmer in the dry season and cooler in the wet season; but the main difference is in the rainfall.

The Old Testament Story and Geography   Not only should the reader of the Bible be able to think correctly about the land of the book, but he should be able to put the book and the land together. The story of the Old Testament can be told as a story of geography and, again, the Bible becomes more meaningful when this aspect is seen. The map on page 156 should be noticed for an understanding of what follows.

The Bible story begins in the Garden of Eden, and this garden is located for us by the rivers Pison, Gihon, Hiddekel, and Euphrates (Genesis 2:8–14). Therefore, on the right side of the map just above the Persian Gulf is where the Bible story starts. It can be seen that this is about seven hundred miles east of the land of Palestine.

Abraham received his call when he was in Ur, and this too is in the same area. Genesis begins the story of the redemption in this land known as the Mesopotamia Valley and then proceeds to bring us to the land of Palestine, with God promising to Abraham this new land.

From the land of Palestine we are taken down to Egypt at the end of Genesis, and it is from this land that the Exodus takes place. In the Book of Exodus the reader is taken from Egypt to the small peninsula of Sinai. It is in this area that the children of Israel wandered for the forty years described in the Book of Numbers.

When we come to Joshua, we are back again in the Promised Land. The main part of the story of the Old Testament is now centered in this area until we come to the second book of Kings. At the end of 2 Kings the nation of Israel has been taken captive by the Assyrians and the Babylonians, and we find the nation almost back where Abraham received his call.

The Old Testament ends with the nation back again in the land of Palestine under Zerubbabel, as recorded in the Books of Ezra and Nehemiah. Thus it can be seen that the story, as seen geographically, is the story of taking the nation from Mesopotamia to Palestine, from Palestine to Egypt, from Egypt to Palestine (via the desert detour), from Palestine to Mesopotamia, and finally from Mesopotamia back to Palestine.

The reader is encouraged to fit the chart on page 155 into his understanding of the geography of the Bible so that as each book is read the exact location is recalled and the place of that book in the overall picture is seen. The more at home you are in the contents of the book, the more you will appreciate the book and, perhaps, the more God will be able to teach you from its pages.

The Gospels and Geography   If the geography of the Old Testament is known, there will be no problem in the geography of the Gospels. The Gospels are very simple in their geography, since they tell the story of Jesus and He spent His time here on earth mostly within the limits of the land of Palestine.

There are, however, certain locations and names that need to be placed in the reader's mind. In order to help in this aspect, there is a map on page 157 on which some of the main locations of the Gospels are marked. These are not exhaustive, but they will serve as a guide so that the reader can recognize where Christ was when a certain event took place.

The Spread of the Gospel and Geography   In the Book of Acts, the Apostle Paul is the God-ordained instrument in spreading the good news of redemption to places and people outside the land of Palestine. In order for the Book of Acts and for the Epistles that fit in this time period to be meaningful geographically, it is necessary to notice the three missionary journeys that Paul took.

Paul's travels took him many miles with the good news that Jesus Christ is God's provision for the redemption from sin. These many miles were traveled, however, in an area that once again is not very large. The reader is encouraged to note the map on page 158 and to notice the area between the eastern end of the Mediterranean Sea and the Black Sea to the north. This area, along with the areas of Greece and Macedonia, is the location of Paul's travels.

The first missionary journey is recorded in Acts 13–14. On this trip Paul went to the Isle of Cyprus, then on to Perga in Pamphylia, Antioch in Pisidia, Iconium, Derbe, Lystra, and then he returned the same way back to Antioch in Syria, except that he did not revisit the Isle of Cyprus.

The second journey is recorded in Acts 15:36–18:22. On this trip Paul went by land to the cities of his first trip, and then went further north until he came to Troas. From Troas he went into Macedonia, and then on into Greece. It was on this journey that churches were established in Philippi, Thessalonica, and Corinth, to mention but a few.

Paul's final missionary journey is found in Acts 18:23–21:3, and this section is a record of Paul revisiting the churches of his second journey. Most of his time he spent in the city of Ephesus. The maps on pages 156 and 158 are given so that the journeys of Paul can be seen at a glance. Keep these places in mind and keep a flow of the geography ever in sight.

Chronology

One can approach the realm of dates with mixed emotions. To be sure, dates of the distant past are not very exciting and, in some cases, are not life-changing. The dates of important events of our past are not really as important as the dates in our future. But the dates in the past are important for fixing events better in our minds and for setting up a sequence of events. The Bible is not an almanac of dates to be viewed with interest and to settle idle arguments. Dates as given in the Bible are provided so that we who did not live in that time might have a better idea of the things that did happen.

Many of the events in the Bible are not dated. Many are dated in such a way as to allow for a variation of date. Where the events of the Bible touch an event recorded by other sources, the dates can be established with more certainty. The dates in this section are given to help see the movement of events and to see the general time period of the events. They are not given as the last word in dating, but merely as guides or helps in understanding the message of the book.

Dates and the Story   Although the story of the Bible begins with the story of creation, it is beyond this writer to attempt to establish any date for the creation of God's universe. The exact age of man and the exact age of the things in this world are not told in the Bible. The Bible establishes the fact and the manner of creation, but it does not establish the date.

The time line on page 155 is an attempt at making the story of the Bible more understandable by seeing the important dates. The time of the *formation* or of Abraham can be set at about 2000 B.C. The date of the Exodus is usually established as between 1550 and 1400 B.C. Thus the deliverance and the wanderings are located in this period. According to Joshua 14:10, there is a period of forty-five years between the experience at Kadesh-barnea, when Israel refused to enter the land, and the time when the land was ready to be divided among the tribes.

The period of the declension is a period of 450 years according to Paul, as recorded in Acts 13:20, and this brings us to 1050 B.C. The first three kings of Israel each ruled for a period of forty years (compare Acts 13:21; 2 Samuel 5:5; 1 Kings 14:42). Therefore, we can place Saul, David, and Solomon in the period around 1000 B.C.

After the first three kings, the nation of Israel divided into two sections. The people of the northern kingdom remained in the land until the year 722 B.C., when Assyria took them captive. The southern section remained for another 116 years until Babylonia took them captive in 606 B.C.

According to Jeremiah 25:1–14; 2 Chronicles 36:29–23; Ezra 1:1–5; and Daniel 9:1–2, the captivity of the southern tribes was for a period of seventy years. From 606 to 536 B.C. the nation of Israel was in Babylon. In 536 B.C. the line again starts for the story is of the nation in the land. This continues for the next 136 years. The nation is in the land and is attempting to reestablish itself. The Old Testament phase of the story thus ends in the year 400 B.C. and the next part of the story does not begin until the year 6 B.C. with the birth of John the Baptizer.

It may seem strange to some that Christ was not born in A.D. 1, since it is His birth that is supposed to be the dividing line for our reckoning of time. The answer to this problem is that those who made our calendars and established many of our past dates were in error because they did not have all the facts. Today we can take a better look at the facts and most agree that the birth of Christ must be placed in the year 6 B.C. In Luke 3:1, the date of the fifteenth year of Tiberius Caesar is used to establish the date for John's ministry and the baptism of Jesus. This brings us to the year A.D. 29, since we can date the reign of Tiberius from A.D. 14 from other sources. The Gospel story about the life and death and resurrection of Christ takes us up to about A.D. 32.

The period from the first Pentecost in the Book of Acts to the death of the Apostle Paul is usually given as from A.D. 32 to A.D. 66/67. Thus the story of the Bible ends (for the most part) with this date. The line can continue until about A.D. 100, with the end of the Apostle John's life, since his books are considered to have been written near the end of his fruitful life.

Thus, the time line can reach from 2000 B.C. to A.D. 100. These are the main dates and by learning these few important dates, the reader of the Word of God will begin to find fresh understanding and meaning to the story.

The Dates and the Books   It is no great problem for the reader of the Bible to place most of the books in their proper sequence once the story of the Bible is known. Also, it is no great problem to fix approximate dates for the contents of most of his books. The key to the dating of most books is a simple one. By looking at the beginning and ending of each historical book or books that tell the story as we have tried to establish, the position of each book in relation to the time line can be seen. Also, by reading the first chapter of each of the other books, their dates can also be fixed so that they can be likewise placed in the line.

The chart on page 155 will show where each book can be placed on the time line, but the reader is encouraged to see this himself by reading the proper place. For example, look at Isaiah 1:1. In this verse we are told that Isaiah prophesied during the reigns of Uzziah, Jotham, Ahaz, and Hezekiah. By noting the list of the kings of Judah it can be seen exactly where Isaiah fits in this period. Since Ahaz was ruling in the south when Assyria took the north captive in 722, it becomes a very small thing to establish the exact date of this book.

In the New Testament the key is the same, except that, rather than looking for a king or such, you need to look at the place of writing or the circumstance of the writer. As an example, when we read 1 Thessalonians 3:1–13, we see that it fits the material starting in Acts 17:15 and thus fits in the period of Paul's second missionary journey.

Do not be afraid of the places and the dates of the Bible. They are given to make you more familiar with the basic story. The more you know and the more you understand about the basic story, the more the book becomes a living book and a book to be enjoyed. Plus, a book to change your life.

4
Historical Books

GENESIS

The Book of Genesis is the book of beginnings. The root meaning of the word *genesis* is "to be born" or "to come into existence." This is the message of the first book of the Bible. The seed plot of the whole Bible is this first book.

The world, man, man's sin, redemption, worship, nations, the nation of Israel, and a revelation of the person of God are a few of the important truths that have their beginnings in this book. Each of these truths as well as the many others should be carefully noted and used as foundations for the truths found in other books of the Bible.

One of the easiest ways to think through this book is to trace the lives of the men described in it. If you can follow Adam, Cain, Noah, Abraham, Isaac, Esau, Jacob, and Joseph, you will have no trouble following the message of this first book. Try to gather certain essentials from each man's life so that the man is real to you. Check his birth, his travels, his failures, his successes, and the revelation of God to each man and see how this helps.

Some of the books of the Bible have authors that are not clearly known to us. Genesis, however, is one of the Five Books of Moses and, as such, can be definitely attributed to him. The common belief of the rest of Scripture points to this fact (see Joshua 1:8; 1 Kings 2:3; Daniel 9:11–13; Matthew 19:8; Romans 10:5).

The story of Genesis begins with the creation of all things.

The story continues through the fall of man and through the constant disobedience of man. From chapter 12 on to the end of the book it is the message of the beginning of Israel. The nation is started with one man, Abraham, and soon starts to grow with the birth of the twelve sons of Jacob. The book ends with the nation of Israel (the family of Jacob) in Egypt.

Chapters 12 through 22 are of extreme importance. In these chapters are recorded God's dealings with Abraham and the promises made to him and through him. The rest of the Old Testament is the carrying out of these promises as well as the promises of the coming of Christ. Some of these promises to Abraham and the nation of Israel are still to be fulfilled and, as such, become important for an understanding of God's dealing with this nation in the present and future.

Outline of the Book of Genesis

    I   The stage of redemption (creation of the world)   1–3
       A   The creation story   1
       B   The creation and fall of man   2–3

   II   The need for redemption (manifestation of sin)   4–11
       A   Murder and death   4–5
       B   Disobedience and judgment   6–9
       C   Rebellion and confusion   10–11

  III   The avenue of redemption
                      (the line of the Redeemer)   12–50
       A   The father of the line (Abraham)   12–23
       B   The son of promise (Isaac)   24–27
       C   The father of the tribes (Jacob)   28–36
       D   The son of deliverance (Joseph)   37–50

EXODUS

For a good understanding of the whole story of the Old Testament, the Book of Exodus is a must. It is in this book that we find the Law given to the nation of Israel, and it is in this book that we find the system of worship God gave to His chosen nation.

The story of Exodus is simple, yet profound. When the book opens, the nation of Israel has grown and finds itself in bondage to Egypt. God raises up a deliverer in the person of Moses, and he leads the people out of Egypt and into the Sinaitic peninsula. While the nation is camped at Mt. Sinai, God gives to them the Law as a system of worship. One half of the book is given to the deliverance (from whence we get the name of the book), and the other half is given to the giving of the Law and the tabernacle.

The easiest way to think through this book is by places and events that happened at these places. By getting Israel from Egypt to Sinai through the Red Sea experience, you will become familiar with the first part of the book. The last half of the book can be understood as the Ten Commandments are learned and as the various parts of the tabernacle are understood.

The tabernacle was given by God to the nation of Israel as a pattern of worship. Israel's life for years centered around this structure. Later the temple replaced the tabernacle and was the permanent house of worship.

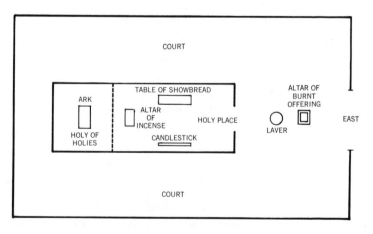

PLAN OF EARLY TABERNACLE

Outline of the Book of Exodus

I   Moses and Pharaoh   1–12
   A   The life and call of Moses   1–4
   B   The contest with Pharaoh   5–12

II   Moses and the people   13–18
   A   Across the sea   13–15:22
   B   Manna and water   15:23–17:7
   C   Victory over circumstances   17:8–17:16
   D   Advice from a father-in-law   18

III   Moses and God   19–40
   A   The Law given   19–24
   B   The tabernacle given   25–31
   C   The Law broken   32–35
   D   The tabernacle built   36–40

Some key words and ideas for the three sections might prove helpful:

1–12	13–18	19–40
Deliverer	Deliverance	Devotion
Triumph	Trip	Tabernacle
Contest	Convoy	Construction
In Egypt	In Desert	At Sinai

LEVITICUS

The Book of Leviticus gets its name from the worship that is described in the book. This worship is often called the Levitical system since it centers around the sons of Levi. This book tells the Israelite how he is to live his life and how he is to carry out his worship of God.

There are many chapters in Leviticus which are important to an understanding of the life of the nation of Israel. The five great sacrifices are found in this book (chapters 1–5). This book is the only one that describes the Day of Atonement (chapter 16). The great feasts of Israel are also listed and described in this book, chapter 23). The reader of the Bible needs to be familiar with these great parts of the life of Israel.

The five sacrifices are: (1) burnt offering, (2) meal offering, (3) peace offering, (4) sin offering, and (5) trespass offering. The first three are called sweet savor offerings since they do not involve sin or its consequence. These are offerings that are to be offered because the worshiper loves God. The last two are called non-sweet savor offerings since they do concern the offerer and his sin (see chapters 1–5).

The great feasts in Israel are: (1) Passover, (2) Unleavened Bread, (3) First Fruits, (4) Pentecost, (5) Trumpets, (6) Atonement, and (7) Tabernacles. The reader is encouraged to study each of these and to see their meaning in the life of Israel past, present, and future.

Outline of the Book of Leviticus

I The worship of the people   1–10
   A   The five offerings   1–5
   B   The laws of the offerings   6–7
   C   The priests   8–9
   D   Nadad and Abihu
               (example of improper worship)   10

II The walk of the people   11–27
   A   Regarding their diet   11
   B   Regarding childbirth   12
   C   Regarding leprosy   13–15
   D   Regarding the Day of Atonement   16–17
   E   Regarding relations with others   18–20
   F   Regarding priests   21–22
   G   Regarding feasts   23
   H   Regarding laws of the land   24–27

NUMBERS

Numbers continues the story of the deliverance of the nation of Israel that was begun in Exodus. Exodus ended after Moses led the people from Egypt to Mt. Sinai. Numbers begins after the tabernacle is built and the people are ready to march for the rest of the distance from Sinai to Palestine.

Perhaps a better name for the book would be that of Marching or Wandering. The name Numbers is valid, however, for twice in the book a census of the fighting men is taken, and it is from this fact that the name is taken (compare chapters 1 and 26). The reason another name is suggested is to let the reader know what the main story of the book is. The nation of Israel spends its time in these pages wandering around the desert area of Sinai because they would not enter the Promised Land when God told them.

The time period of Numbers is the famed forty years, to which reference is often made. This refers to the time it took Israel to get from Egypt to Palestine. The time is long because of rebellion, not because of distance. Forty is the number God chose for them to take since the representatives took forty days to spy the land, as recorded in chapters 13 and 14. They had already spent two years in the desert at Sinai building the tabernacle and getting organized for the trip through the desert; so for thirty-eight years they had to "wander" to fulfill this judgment.

It is interesting to calculate the number of people that were in the nation at this time. According to chapter 1:46 there were 603,550 men that were over twenty and could go to war. This did not include men in the tribe of Levi, nor did it include those men under twenty or the women and children. A conservative estimate might be in the neighborhood of two to three million. At the end of the wanderings the number of fighting men was 601,730. Thus, the number remained fairly constant although God's judgment was that all over twenty at the time of the rebellion (chapter 14) would die in the wilderness (with the exception of Caleb and Joshua).

A matter of interest as well as an opportunity to learn the tribes of Israel is the organization of the camp. God is the God of order and not confusion; so this large group of people had to be organized both in their camp and in their march. These facts are recorded in chapters 2 through 10, and a diagram of the appearance of the camp would be as follows:

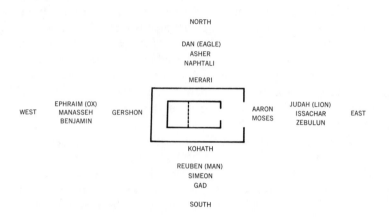

Outline of the Book of Numbers

I   Preparation for the journey   1–10:10
   A   Numbering   1
   B   Encampment   2
   C   Levites   3–4
   D   People   5–8
   E   Passover   9
   F   Trumpets   10:1–10

II   First phase of the journey   10:11–14:45
   A   Failures from Sinai to Kadesh   10:11–12:26
   B   Failures at Kadesh   13–14

III   Detour in the journey   15–20
   A   Promise of completion   15
   B   Sin of Korah   16
   C   The rod of Aaron   17–18
   D   The heifer for cleansing   19
   E   The death of Miriam and Aaron   20

IV   Second phase of the journey   21–36
    A   Experience with the serpents   21
    B   Experience with Balaam   22–25
    C   New numbering   26
    D   New leader   27
    E   New instructions   28–32
    F   Summary of the journey   33
    G   Preparation for entry into the land   34–36

DEUTERONOMY

The fifth book of Moses is the Book of Deuteronomy. This completes the writings of Moses and concludes the set known as the Pentateuch. Deuteronomy gets its name from the fact that this book is a regiving of the Law in preparation for the new generation to live in the land. In that sense it is a deuter/onomy, or second Law.

There are some interesting words that are common in this book. The words *keep, obey,* and *learn* all occur with a frequency that does not occur in the other books of Moses. The word *love* is found in this book more than in all the other books of the Law put together.

The word *remember* is perhaps the key word of the book. This word is found thirteen times (5:15; 7:18; 8:2, 18; 9:7, 27; 15:15; 16:3, 12; 24:9, 18; 25:17; 32:7). In these passages the nation is called upon to remember their past, God's performance, and God's person. These are three things for all people to keep in remembrance if they wish to remain strong in God.

Deuteronomy should be easy for the student since the main portion of the book is review. Moses spends most of this book reviewing either the Law and its application to the people or the journey from Sinai to the plains of Moab.

Outline of the Book of Deuteronomy

I   Reviewing the journeys   1–4   (the past)
    A   From Sinai to Kadesh   1

    B   From Kadesh to Moab   2–3

    C   Lessons for the entry   4

II   Reviewing the Law   5–26   (the present)

    A   The Law taught and to be taught   5–6

    B   The Command to be separate   7

    C   Commands to be followed   8–12

    D   Instructions for life in the land   13–26

III Reviewing the future   27–30   (the future)

    A   The blessings and the cursings   27

    B   Promises in keeping with obedience   28

    C   The promise of the land   29–30

IV   Reviewing Moses' last days   31–34

    A   Counsel to Levites and Joshua   31

    B   Song of Jehovah   32

    C   Blessing of the nation   33

    D   Death of Moses   34

JOSHUA

The story that was started in Exodus and continued in Numbers is brought to a conclusion in Joshua. Deuteronomy 6:23 records that God brought Israel out of Egypt so that He might bring them into Palestine. In Joshua the nation of Israel is brought into the land of promise, and in this book the land is theirs to be divided and owned.

Joshua is one of the great men of the Old Testament. He was one of the twelve spies sent into the land from Kadeshbarnea, and he and Caleb were the only ones to believe God. He was chosen by God to be the successor to Moses and was throughout the wilderness travels a constant help to Moses (Exodus 17:9; 24:13; 32:17; 33:11; Numbers 13–14; 27:18; 34:17).

The spiritual lessons that can be learned from this book are many. Success in the spiritual realm is clearly seen in this book even though the text has to do with success in the physical realm. The way of victory as outlined for Joshua in chapter 1 is certainly the way of victory for everyone. A study of this book and a study of the truths of the spiritual life can go hand in hand.

The nation of Israel is finally back in her land. God has promised to Abraham that this land would be his and his seed's after him. The nation spent many long years in Egypt, and then those years in the wilderness when the land looked so close, yet so far. Now in this book God goes before them and defeats their enemies so that they can enter, conquer, and divide that land for their own. The events in this book are all within a short time. From the entry of the nation into the land to the death of Joshua is all that this book records. The time period is around thirty years.

Outline of the Book of Joshua

I   Entering the land   1–5
   A   The way to success   1
   B   The power for success   2–4
   C   The people for success   5:1–12
   D   The captain for success   5:13–15

II   Conquering the land   6–12
   A   Central campaign   6–9
   B   Southern campaign   10
   C   Northern campaign   11
   D   Summary of the battles   12

III   Dividing the land   13–21
   A   Reuben, Gad, Manasseh   13
   B   Caleb   14
   C   Judah   15
   D   The rest   16–19
   E   Cities of refuge   20
   F   Levites   21

IV   Enjoying the land   22–24
   A   No divisions   22
   B   No transgressions   23
   C   No idols   24

JUDGES

The darkest period in Israel's history is perhaps the period known as the period of the judges. This time is marked by repeated departures from the Lord and by repeated judgments by the Lord. This is the time in Israel's history when "every man did that which was right in his own eyes" (Judges 21:25).

To understand this book it is first necessary to understand what has been called the cycle in the book. This cycle or repeated set of events occurs a number of times in the book and is outlined in 2:11–19. The cycle is:

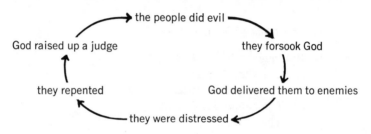

While the judge was alive and leading it, the nation would follow God. But as soon as the judge died, the nation would go away from God again.

It is advantageous to notice that the same information occurs in each case of the cycle. The oppressor, the length of time Israel was oppressed, the judge, and the length of time the judge was helping Israel are indicated. As an example, note 3:5–11. The enemy is Mesopotamia. The servitude was for eight years. The judge was Othniel, and he ruled or judged for forty years. It would be helpful to make a chart showing the rest of the cycles and the information that is given for each one.

The time period of the Book of Judges is four hundred and fifty years, according to Paul in Acts 13:20. It is very possible that the judges were not judges of the whole nation, and thus it is possible that the judges overlapped in their ministry. This means that one judge could be delivering a part of Israel from their enemies while another judge was delivering another section of Israel from their oppressor. The time period covered would be four hundred years, but the judges may not account for each year of this time.

Outline of the Book of Judges

I The cause for declension   1–2
   A Incomplete victory   1
   B Incomplete affection   2

II The path of declension   3–16
   A Othniel   3:1–11
   B Ehud   3:12–31
   C Deborah-Barak   4–5
   D Gideon   6–8:32
   E Abimelech   8:33–9:57
   F Jephthah   10–12
   G Samson   13–16

III The results of declension   17–21
   A In the religious realm   17–18
   B In the moral realm   19
   C In the political realm   20–21

RUTH

One of the most beautiful stories in the Bible is the story of Ruth. This is also one of the most beautiful stories in literature anywhere. The unfolding of the events in this book is simply done, yet it is done with a beauty that is hard to copy.

The brightness of this book is seen more clearly by the fact that the events recorded in this narrative are events that occur during the dark period of the judges (1:1). We are shown thereby that while the period is indeed a dark one, it is also one where individuals were in right relation to God and were doing as He would have them to do.

The value of this book is at least threefold. It is interesting in that it shows some of the cultural and moral life of the times.

This is the clearest description of the practices of reaping and threshing, as well as the custom for handling the major affairs of the cities. Further, this book is important for it shows as no other book the actual carrying out of the practice of the kinsman-redeemer, as described in Leviticus 25. Not the least of the values of this book is the fact that it shows how a major part of the genealogy of Christ was carried on. In chapter 4, verses 17 through 22, we find perhaps the main reason for the book—to bring us further along in the line of the Redeemer.

Outline of the Book of Ruth

    I   Ruth in Moab   1:1–18
        A   Elimelech leaving   1:1–5
        B   Orphah leaving   1:6–14
        C   Ruth leaving   1:15–18

   II   Ruth in Bethlehem   1:19–2:25
        A   Return to Bethlehem   1:19–22
        B   Request to glean   2:1–7
        C   Reward to Ruth   2:8–13
        D   Refreshment for Ruth   2:14–16
        E   Report to Naomi   2:17–23

  III   Ruth in the threshing floor   3:1–18
        A   Naomi's desire   3:1–5
        B   Boaz' decision   3:6–13
        C   Ruth's declaration   3:14–18

  IV   Ruth in Boaz' house   4:1–22
        A   Rehearsal of the facts   4:1–6
        B   Redemption of Ruth   4:7–12
        C   Restorer of life   4:13–17
        D   Results of the marriage   4:18–22

1 SAMUEL

In the Book of 1 Samuel we find a real transition. Samuel was the last of the judges. It is true that he made his sons judges after him, but we read of no activity on their part except that of perverting judgment (8:1–3). Also, in this book we are brought to the first king of the nation of Israel. The office of king will be the main office for the rest of the Old Testament, and all events and times will be reckoned by the king on the throne at the time.

The Book of Samuel is a book of contrast in individuals. Eli is in contrast to Samuel; Saul is in contrast to David; and the sons of Eli and Samuel are in contrast to Jonathan, the son of Saul. The reader will do well to notice the things recorded of each of these men.

As the Books of Samuel and Kings are read, it will help to refer to the list of the kings in an earlier chapter so that the reader will not become confused by the many men and just where the particular man fits into the scheme of Israel's history.

The Book of Samuel becomes of vast importance when it is remembered that our Lord is to sit on the throne of David and that He is called the son of David. It is the Book of 1 Samuel that brings us to this important man, David, although it is the Book of 2 Samuel that gives us the details of his reign.

A word needs to be said about the author. It is evident that Samuel could not have written all of 1 Samuel, and certainly none of 2 Samuel, since he died before the events of 1 Samuel are completed. The books obtain their name from the principal personage of the first book rather than the writer of the book, as in the case in many of the other books of the Old and New Testaments. We are not sure of the author of these books nor of the books of Kings and Chronicles, but it is certain that "holy men of God spake as they were moved by the Holy Ghost" (2 Peter 1:21).

Outline of the Book of 1 Samuel

I   Eli and Samuel   1–8
   A   The birth of Samuel   1
   B   The judgment on Eli   2
   C   The commission of Samuel   3
   D   The death of Eli and ministry of Samuel   4–7
   E   The request for a king   8

II Samuel and Saul 9–15
  A Saul chosen 9
  B Saul anointed 10
  C Kingdom established 11–12
  D Sins of Saul 13–15

III Saul and David 16–31
  A David chosen 16
  B David and Goliath 17
  C Saul vs. David 18–26
  D David with the Gentiles 27–30
  E The death of Saul 31

2 SAMUEL

The Book of 2 Samuel is devoted to the reign of David as king over Israel. The importance of this man and the events are thus set apart, since there is no other man that has one whole book devoted to his rule.

Since David ruled for a total of forty years, this book covers only that period. These forty years begin with Israel as a nation divided and in subjection to their enemies. As the reign of David unfolds, the nation is gradually united under him. Israel's enemies suffered defeat after defeat at David's hands, so that, by the end of his lifetime, she was chief among the nations.

The Davidic covenant that is recorded in chapter 7 is another of the important covenants that God has established with the nation of Israel and shows what God plans to do with this people. It is this promise to the nation that helps establish the great fact of the kingdom to come when Christ will sit on the throne of his father David and rule over the house of Israel.

As one reads the accounts of the life of David in this book, it becomes somewhat of a question why God would call him a man after His own heart. The answer may be that 2 Samuel is recording the events and actions while the Book of Psalms is where one must go to see the heart of the man. In Psalms we see a man who truly was a sinner, but we see a man who knew what his sin did to God and to him. David not only knew the effects of his sin, but he knew what God required to be clean in His sight. In this sense, David was a man after God's own heart.

There are many characters in the Book of 2 Samuel, and as their identity is known, it will aid in understanding the book. The following are suggested as basic: David, Abner, Ishbosheth, Joab, Uzzah, Nathan, Mephibosheth, Bathsheba, Uriah, Amnon, Tamar, Absalom, Ahithophel, Hushai, Zadok, Amasa, Ziba, Shimei, Araunah.

Outline of the Book of 2 Samuel

I The triumphs of David   1–10
   A King in Hebron   1–4   Establishment of unity
   B King in Jerusalem   5–10   Enlarging of borders

II The troubles of David   11–21
   A Sins with Bathsheba   11–12
   B Amnon and Absalom   13–14
   C Absalom and David   15–19
   D Internal strife   20–21

III The testimony of David   22–24
   A His song of deliverance   22
   B His list of mighty men   23
   C His heart of love   24

1 KINGS

First Kings is the book that records for us the reign of Solomon and also the division of the kingdom. Both of these are important for a knowledge of the history of the nation of Israel and for an understanding of the program of the line of the Redeemer. It is in this book that the temple is built, replacing the tabernacle built in the desert under Moses.

Another important feature of this book is found in the material given about Elijah. Up to this time the Bible has recorded activities of a prophet, but they have been activities that centered around another person. With the ministry of Elijah, we are brought for the first time to the activities of the man himself, and others are seen in relation to him. From this time on, prophets will play an important role in the history of the nation.

The reader of the Bible will do well to fix the major facts of the division of the kingdom in his mind. The rest of the story of the Old Testament is built around these facts, and if they are not known the Bible may become confusing. Most of the important details are recorded in chapter 12. As you read this chapter notice: the two divisions—north, called Israel, and south, called Judah or the house of David; the first two kings—Rehoboam in the south and Jeroboam in the north; the two capitals—Jerusalem in the south and Samaria in the north; the two religions—the true in the south and the false in the north; the tribes involved—Judah, Benjamin, and Levi, with a remnant from the rest, in the south and the other ten tribes in the north.

For future orientation we need to remember that Solomon wrote Proverbs, Ecclesiastes, and Song of Solomon; they were written during the first part of this book. Beginning with 1 Kings, the reader of the Bible needs to think of the other books that belong to the same period (see p. 155).

Outline of the Book of 1 Kings

I   The death of David   1:1–2:12
   A   David's sickness,   1:1–4
   B   David's successor   1:5–53
   C   David's charge   2:1–9
   D   David's death   2:10–12

II   The dominion of Solomon   2:13–11:43
   A   Solomon's first actions   2:13–46
   B   Solomon's choice   3
   C   Solomon's weath and wisdom   4
   D   Solomon's labors   5–8
   E   Solomon's kingdom   9–10
   F   Solomon's folly   11

III The division of the kingdom   12:1–16:28
   A   Forming the break   12
   B   Jeroboam (Israel)   13–14:20
   C   Rehoboam (Judah)   14:21–31
   D   Abijam (Judah)   15:1–8
   E   Asa (Judah)   15:9-24
   F   Nadab (Israel)   15:25–32
   G   Baash (Israel)   15:33–16:7
   H   Elah (Israel)   16:8–14
   I   Zimri (Israel)   16:15–20
   J   Omri (Israel)   16:21–28

IV The declarations of Elijah   16:29–22:53
   A   Ahab's sins   16:24–34
   B   Elijah and the famine   17
   C   Elijah and the prophets of Baal   18
   D   Elijah and God   19
   E   Ahab's victories   20
   F   Ahab and Naboth's vineyard   21
   G   Ahab and Jehoshaphat   22

2 KINGS

In the Hebrew Bible the double books are single, so that 1 and 2 Samuel, 1 and 2 Kings, and 1 and 2 Chronicles are each one book. Just as 2 Samuel continues the story of 1 Samuel, so 2 Kings continues the story of 1 Kings. In fact, it might be said that the story begun in 1 Samuel (the kingdom) is brought to a close in 2 Kings, for it is in this book that the two divisions of the kingdom are taken into captivity.

First Kings covers about one hundred twenty years with about forty of these being the reign of King Solomon. Second Kings covers a period of three hundred years, from the translation of Elijah to the captivity of the southern kingdom.

There is no easy way to think through this book since it is a collection of the activities of the many kings of the two divisions. Again, the best thing a reader can do is to keep a list of the kings before him so that the many names do not become meaningless.

The time and people of the two captivities in this book are important for the Bible reader. Assyria, with its capital in Nineveh, took the northern tribes (Israel) into captivity in the year 722 B.C. The final overthrow and destruction of Jerusalem was in the year 586 B.C., and each of these dates is important. The year 722 is important since it marks the beginning of the judgment of God upon His people and the time when only one of the kingdoms is left on the scene.

The year 606 is important since it marks the beginning of the seventy years of captivity announced by Jeremiah the prophet (Jeremiah 25). The importance of 586 is that it marks the desolation of the city, which was also to last for seventy years.

The reader is referred to the chart on page 155 to notice that it is during this book and this period that most of the prophetic books were written. The writing prophets probably began with Joel about 850 B.C., and they are still on the scene when the Old Testament closes. It is striking to notice how many voices God raised up to stem the tide of rebellion as judgment came closer.

Outline of the Book of 2 Kings

I   The last days of Elijah   1:1–2:11
   A   Elijah and King Ahaziah   1
   B   Elijah's translation   2:1–11

II   The ministry of Elisha   2:12–9:10
   A   Vindication of the prophet   2:12–25
   B   Elisha and Jehoshaphat   3
   C   Elisha's miracles   4–7
   D   Elisha and Jehoram   8
   E   Anointing of Jehu   9:1–10

III   The last days of the divided kingdom   9:11–17:41
   A   Jehu (Israel)   9:11–10:36
   B   Athaliah (Judah)   11

68

C   Jehoash (Judah)   12
D   Jehoahaz (Israel)   13:1–19
E   Jehoash (Israel)13:10–25
F   Amaziah (Judah)   14:1–22
G   Jeroboam II (Israel)   14:23–29
H   Azariah (Judah)   15:1–7
I   Zechariah (Israel)   15:8–12
J   Shallum (Israel)   15:13–15
K   Menahem (Israel)   15:16–22
L   Pekahiah (Israel)   15:23–26
M   Pekah (Israel)   15:27–31
N   Jotham (Judah)   15:32–36
O   Ahaz (Judah)   16
P   Hoshea (Israel)   17

IV   The last days of the single kingdom   18–25
     A   Hezekiah   18:1–20:21
     B   Manasseh   21:1–26
     C   Josiah   22:1–23:30
     D   Jehoahaz   23:31–33
     E   Jehoiakim   23:34–24:6
     F   Jehoiachin   24:7–16
     G   Zedekiah   24:17–25:7
     H   Final captivity   25:8–30

1 AND 2 CHRONICLES

The events covered by the two books now before us are events that are covered for the most part by either Samuel or Kings. The question then is why should there be another book with the same material? There is no easy answer to this question, but perhaps there can be a suggestion.

The previous books record the history as it unfolded with no particular emphasis on one section of the division. Chronicles, however, does not record the events relating to the northern kingdom. Again, it is noticed that a great deal is made of the genealogies of the people and that the spiritual relationships are brought to the fore. As an example, from 2 Kings we would not know of the spiritual revival of King Manasseh; but Chronicles records this fact (2 Chronicles 33). The conclusion is then that these books are the priests' records of the southern kingdom and stress the spiritual qualities of this period. The book is of special importance for the genealogical records that were so much a part of Israel's history and also of our Lord's qualifications for the throne.

Outline of the Book of 1 Chronicles

I   Genealogies   1–9
  A   Adam to sons of Esau   1
  B   Sons of Israel   2
  C   Sons of sons of Israel   3–8
  D   Miscellaneous   9

II   Saul   10
  A   The suicide of Saul   10:1–6
  B   The shame of Saul   10:7–12
  C   The sins of Saul   10:13–14

III   David   11–29
  A   David made king   11:1–9
  B   David's mighty men   11:10–12:40
  C   The curse of the ark   13
  D   Victory over the Philistines   14
  E   The blessing of the ark   15:1–16:43
  F   David's desire   17
  G   Victories over surrounding kings   18–20
  H   Sin of numbering the people   21
  I   Preparation of the temple   22–27
  J   David's last words   28–29

Outline of the Book of 2 Chronicles

I   The reign of Solomon   1–9
  A   Prayer for wisdom   1
  B   Preparation for the temple   2
  C   Plan for the temple   3–4

    D   Dedication of the temple   5–7
    E   Fame of Solomon   8–9

II The division of the kingdom   10–12
    A   Forsaken counsel   10:1–11
    B   Jeroboam's rebellion   10:12–19
    C   Initial strifes   11
    D   Rehoboam's sin   12

III The kings of Judah   13–35
    A   Abijah   13
    B   Asa   14–16
    C   Jehoshaphat   17–20
    D   Jehoram   21
    E   Ahaziah   22:1–9
    F   Athaliah   22:10–23:21
    G   Joash   24
    H   Amaziah   25
    I   Uzziah   26
    J   Jotham   27
    K   Ahaz   28
    L   Hezekiah   29–32
    M   Manasseh   33:1–20
    N   Amon   33:21–25
    O   Josiah   34–35

IV The final overthrow   36
    A   Jehoahaz by Egypt   36:1–4
    B   Jehoiakim by Babylon   36:5–8
    C   Jehoiachin by Babylon   36:9–10
    D   Zedekiah by Babylon   36:11–21
    E   A ray of hope   36:22–23

EZRA

Approximately seventy years passed between the time 2 Kings ended and Ezra began. The Book of Ezra is the first of the postexilic (after the exile or captivity) books. These books

(Ezra, Esther, Nehemiah, Haggai, Zechariah, Malachi) relate the experiences of the nation as it came back to the land and started to be a nation under God again.

Ezra is a very interesting person. It is he that is often made to be the writer of various historical books of the Old Testament since he is by occupation a scribe of the Law (Ezra 7:6). He is a man that is noted for his attention to and interest in the Word of God. Almost every time his name is mentioned it is in connection with the Word.

When Babylon destroyed Jerusalem, the magnificent temple of Solomon was stripped and burned. When the Jews returned to their land by permission of King Cyrus of Persia, they wanted to establish the temple first. The Book of Ezra is the record of this struggle to first erect the temple and then to get the people in right relation to God and to His Law.

Since the Books of Ezra, Esther, and Nehemiah make mention of a number of Persian kings, it is important that these men be placed in proper time and sequence. The following is a list of the first kings of Persia with their dates and where they fit in the history of Israel.

Cyrus	550–530	Allowed Israel to return
Cambyses	530–521	Stopped the work of the temple
Darius I	521–486	Allowed work to continue
Xerxes I	486–465	King Ahasuerus in Book of Esther
Artaxerxes I	465–424	Return of Nehemiah
Darius II	424–404	
Artaxerxes II	404–358	

Outline of the Book of Ezra

I   Zerubbabel and his work—the temple   1–6
   A   Decree for the return   1
   B   People who returned   2
   C   Worship of the people   3:1–7
   D   Work of the people   3:8–13
   E   Hinderance to the work   4
   F   Encouragement to work   5
   G   Completion of the temple   6

II   Ezra and his work—the people   7–10
   A   The man Ezra   7
   B   The people   8:1–21
   C   The return   8:22–36
   D   Separation of the people   9–10

NEHEMIAH

The story of the remnant and their return to Palestine is finished in the Book of Nehemiah. The temple was rebuilt under Zerubbabel and the people were properly related to God in the first few years of the return. The city of Jerusalem, however, was not really established. The people had built their own homes, but the city as a city with its walls was not rebuilt. (The walls of the ancient cities were very important. A city was not considered autonomous unless it had walls sufficient for its protection. If Jerusalem was to be a major city, it must have its walls rebuilt.) It was Nehemiah that caused the work on the walls to be done, and it is this work which is recorded in this book.

Where Ezra can be described as a man of the Word, it is easy to mark Nehemiah as a man of prayer. His example of a life of prayer for all and any circumstance is certainly worth copying and studying.

In chapter 2, there is a date that becomes very important for the student of the Bible. The twentieth year of Artaxerxes can be firmly established as 445 B.C., and it is this date that becomes the beginning of the seventy weeks as recorded in Daniel. God is very careful to record this date for us so that we can know for certain of His prophetic clock for the nation of Israel and for His Son, our Lord.

Outline of the Book of Nehemiah

  I   The remembrance of Nehemiah   1–2
   A   Prayer to Jehovah   1
   B   Plea to the king   2:1–8
   C   Plan for the work   2:9–20

73

II The rebuilding of the walls   3–7
    A   Record of the builders   3
    B   Response to opposition   4–6
    C   Registering the people   7

III The revival among the people   8–13
    A   The Law read   8
    B   Prayer of confession   9
    C   Reforms instituted   10–11
    D   Dedication of the walls   12
    E   Final reforms   13

ESTHER

Esther is a unique book of the Bible. As one reads these twelve chapters, one becomes aware that the name of God is conspicuous by its absence. This book and the Song of Solomon are the two books of the Bible that do not mention God's name. What makes this book different from Song of Solomon, and thus unique, is that there is ample occasion for God to be brought into the narrative, but He is not.

The fact that God does not find a place in this book has caused some to say that it does not belong in the Bible. Over against this opinion is the fact that the Jews hold this book in the highest regard even to the point of saying that it will remain along with the Torah in the Messianic age.

Probably in no other book is God's hand so evident even though His name is missing. This book shows that God is constantly looking after the nation that is called by His name (Israel—Prince of God), and He will ever work to preserve this people. Certainly, had the plot of Haman in this book been carried out, there would have been no line for the birth of Jesus.

This book has a very important significance to the Jewish people since it is this book that records the beginning of the feast of Purim. The feast of Purim is one of the feasts of the nation of Israel that is celebrated each year. This feast does not seem to be a God-ordained feast like the ones in Leviticus 23, but it is a feast that has its basis in the experience of Scripture.

Outline of the Book of Esther

    I Esther's inauguration   1–2
       A Displacing of Vashti   1
       B Deciding on Esther   2

   II Haman's declaration   3
       A Reason for his wrath   3:1–6
       B Request to the king   3:7–11
       C Recording the declaration   3:12–15

  III Israel's preservation   4–8
       A Fasting by the Jews   4
       B Courage of Esther   5
       C Mordecai exalted   6
       D Haman hanged   7
       E Preservation arranged   8

   IV Purim's installation   9–10
       A Victory for Israel   9:1–10
       B Rest for the Jews   9:11–16
       C Feast recognized   9:17–32
       D Mordecai rewarded   10:1–3

5
Poetical Books

JOB

The Books of Job, Psalms, Proverbs, Ecclesiastes, Song of Solomon, and Lamentations are all poetical books. This title is often confusing to the reader since they do not look like any poetry that we know. There is no English rhyme to these books. The secret is that Hebrew poetry is not rhyme in word sounds, but is a structure built on ideas expressed in the words. This arrangement is called parallelism, and there are three main types with a number of other variations.

One form is often called *completive*. This means that the second line of a verse completes or complements the first line. The two lines are saying virtually the same thing, but in slightly different words (see Psalms 15:1).

A second form is often called *contrastive*, and this kind is most prevalent in the Book of Proverbs. As the name implies, the second line is a different thought from the first (see Proverbs 10:1).

The last major type can be called *constructive*. This type builds upon the first line. The first and third types are similar, but the key to their differences is that the third builds or adds more to the thought expressed in the first. As you read the poetic books, look for these structures.

Job is the first of the poetic books in our English Bible, and this is most likely the best place for the book. The book evidences an early date since no references are made to Israel, the Law, the tabernacle, and since Job is seen as the priest of the family, the latter being an arrangement that was operative in the days of the patriarchs (Abraham, Isaac, and Jacob). It is very possible that this book was written before Moses wrote any of the Pentateuch, and it could therefore be the first book of the Bible. It is also possible that the events or story of Job were oral tradition up to the time of Moses and that Moses, under the direction of God, wrote them down. We are not sure of the author of the book, and so we cannot be sure of the date. But all the evidence seems to point to an early date.

The Book of Job unfolds like a great drama. There is a fine list of characters to be understood and a complete drama with three great acts. The characters are Job, his wife, Satan, Eliphaz (a man of experience), Bildad (a man of tradition), Zophar (a man of dogmatism), Elihu (a young man with insight), and, of course, God.

The story is a simple one in that the three acts are clearly set forth. In the first act we find Job undergoing some very severe testing and losing all that he possesses. In the second act Job is "comforted" by his three friends, Eliphaz, Bildad, and Zophar. This act unfolds by showing us three distinct rounds of debate between each man and Job. The final act is introduced by the man Elihu speaking to Job. Then God speaks to bring the drama to a close.

The main theme of the book is often taken as a discussion of why there is suffering. This is very true. But it seems that the main idea of the book is to show the greatness of God in every circumstance. The answer to any suffering or to any question is to have confidence in the God of the universe.

Outline of the Book of Job

    I   Job in the hands of Satan   1–2:10
        A   The man Job   1:1–5
        B   The first test of Satan   1:6–22
        C   The second test of Satan   2:1–8
        D   The man Job   2:9–10

    II   Job in the hands of men   2:11–31:40
        A   Job's soliloquy   3

      B   First round of debate   4–14
      C   Second round of debate   15–21
      D   Third round of debate   22–31

III   Job in the hand of God   32–42
      A   Preparation by Elihu   32–37
      B   Revelation by God   38–42:6
      C   Vindication of Job   42:7–17

PSALMS

Certainly one of the most loved books of the Bible is the Book of Psalms. This book has been a comfort to the saints since the time it was written. This book as no other gives the expression of the heart of the saint to his God. No matter what the experience of the believer is at the time, there is a psalm or a part of one that will say just what is needed.

The Book of Psalms cannot really be outlined since it is a collection of 150 separate psalms; but there is an arrangement to the book. There are five complete sections or divisions to the 150 chapters. Each division is noticeable by the fact that there is a special doxology at the end of all but the last division. The divisions are:

$$
\begin{array}{rcl}
1 & - & 41 \\
42 & - & 72 \\
73 & - & 89 \\
90 & - & 106 \\
107 & - & 150 \\
\end{array}
$$

Many reasons have been offered for these divisions, but it is hard to find just the exact reason for them. Perhaps one of the best suggestions is that the five divisions parallel the Five Books of Moses. Since the Pentateuch formed the basis of all Jewish thinking, it is very possible that the collection of these psalms was built around this idea.

The Book of Psalms was not written by any one man. It is often called the Psalms of David, but he is just one of the authors. To be sure, he wrote most of the psalms, and it is probably to him that we owe the first collection of them. But other men also had a part in writing these great hymns. The writers are:

David (73 psalms)—3–9; 11–32; 34–41; 51–65; 68–70; 86; 101; 103; 108–110; 122; 124; 131; 133; 138–145
Asaph (12 psalms)—50; 73–83
Sons of Korah (11 psalms)—42; 44–49; 84; 85; 87; 88
Solomon (2 psalms)—72; 127
Ethan (1 psalm)—89
Moses (1 psalm)—90

These writers are found by noting the inscriptions of the various psalms. Two more psalms are ascribed to David by the New Testament: Psalm 2 by Acts 4:25, and Psalm 95 by Hebrews 4:7. This leaves less than fifty psalms that do not have known authors. Many of these may have been written by David or at least written during his time since he was greatly concerned with the worship of God.

For a better understanding of the psalms themselves and for a better understanding of the worship of Israel, it is suggested that the reader take time to look up the various words that are in the inscriptions before the psalms. In this area the book *The Titles to the Psalms* by James William Thirtle is very good.

Since the Book of Psalms does not lend itself to outlining, a list of some of the groups of psalms is helpful.

Types of Psalms

National Psalms occasioned by the events of national life: 14, 44, 46–48, 53, 66, 68, 74, 76, 79, 80, 83, 87, 108, 122, 124–126, 129.

Historical Psalms rehearse passages from the nation's history: 78, 81, 105, 106, 114.

Messianic Psalms speak of the Messiah and of His Kingdom: 2, 8, 16, 22, 24, 35, 40, 41, 68, 69, 72, 87, 89, 97, 102, 118, 132.

Penitential Psalms refer to some occasion of intense sorrow for sin and turning to God: 6, 32, 38, 51, 102, 130, 143.

Imprecatory Psalms call down judgment upon God's enemies: 35, 52, 58, 69, 109, 137, 140.

Hallelujah Psalms begin with "Praise Ye the Lord": 106, 111–113, 117, 135, 146–150.

Thanksgiving Psalms: 105, 107, 118, 136.

The Hallel or Praise Psalms sung at Passover: 113–118.

Psalms of Ascents (origin and use not clearly known): 120–134.

Psalms of the Law: 1, 19, 119.

Acrostic Psalms begin each line by using the next letter in the Hebrew alphabet: 9, 10, 25, 34, 37, 111, 112, 119, 145.

PROVERBS

The Book of Psalms is a book for the worship of the believer. The Book of Proverbs is a guide for the walk of the believer. The Book of Psalms is for the church (temple), while the Book of Proverbs is for the home and for the shop. By definition, a proverb is a short sentence conveying some moral truth or practical lesson in a concise, pointed form. The Book of Proverbs is a collection of these God-given lessons.

Solomon is taken to be the main author of the Book of Proverbs; or at least he is the author of the proverbs, while others helped gather and collect them into a book. Certainly Solomon was qualified from the human point of view to write these proverbs since he was a very wise man. In 1 Kings 4:32 it is stated that Solomon composed three thousand proverbs. The Book of Proverbs contains about five hundred separate proverbs.

The key word to the Book of Proverbs is the word *wisdom*. This word or words like it are the full thrust of the book. God wants His children to *know* how they are to live in this world. The key phrase is *the fear of the Lord* (see 1:29; 2:5, 3:7,

8:13; 9:10; 10:27; 14:26, 27; 15:16, 33; 16:6; 19:23; 22:4; 23:17). This is not meant to carry the idea of fear in the sense of dread, but fear in the sense of respect. The same word is translated *reverence* in the Old Testament (compare Leviticus 19:30; 26:2; Psalms 89:7; 111:9). The way to walk in this life is to *know* that God is to be *respected* or *reverenced* in all we do.

The Book of Proverbs, like Solomon himself, talks about many things. A very interesting way to study this book is to make a list of the verses that deal with a given subject and then to understand the teaching relating to this area. Subjects such as business, children, riches, women, drink, the heart, pride, the tongue, a fool, truth, are worthy of investigation in this book.

Like Psalms, Proverbs is not an easy book to outline. This book is not meant to be understood as a whole, but rather to be understood in its parts. It is more important to know the lesson of the proverbs rather than the structure of Proverbs.

Again, like the Book of Psalms, Proverbs divides into certain clear sections. These sections are marked by a phrase that shows a different collector or purpose. Each section is also marked by a change in the structure of the collection.

Outline of the Book of Proverbs

I Praise of wisdom 1–9
This section is not the usual structure of a proverb. These chapters and verses can be grouped into paragraphs like prose writing. In this section Solomon sets the proper path for his "son" to follow.

II Proverbs for life 10–24
This section is more what we think of when Proverbs is mentioned. Each verse is a different proverb, and there is for the most part no relation between one proverb and the next.

III Principles of order 25–29
The proverbs in this section are grouped in an order.

A subject is discussed by a number of individual proverbs.

IV Praise of virtue   30–31
These last two chapters are ascribed to different people, and they are both proverbs of virtue. Chapter 30 sets forth virtue in life, and chapter 31 sets forth virtue in a woman.

ECCLESIASTES

The Book of Ecclesiastes is entitled "Koheleth" in the Hebrew Bible. This word is translated "the preacher," or one who addresses an assembly, in 1:1 and 1:12. The English word "Ecclesiastes" is the Greek name given to the book in the Septuagint as being the interpretation of the Hebrew word "Koheleth." Thus, the words of this book become the admonition of a preacher to a congregation. These are words to be listened to from a man who knows what he is talking about.

Tradition has consistently established Solomon as the author of this book. His name does not occur in the book; but the experiences, written in the first person, are the experiences of Solomon. The writer is seen as king of Israel (1:12), as possessing great wisdom (1:16), as possessing great wealth (2:1–11), and as one who has had the opportunity to observe one thousand women (7:28). If Solomon is not the author, we have no idea of the identity of the one who wrote this book.

It is important to notice the theme and the purpose of this book. The book constantly shows us the theme by the phrase "vanities of vanities." According to this book, there is nothing that can satisfy the heart of man. The purpose of the book seems to be to give us an earthly view of the barrenness of all that this life can offer. God allows a man who has tried all things to write his conclusion of the emptiness of this life.

It must be remembered that this book is man speaking out of his experiences and, unless the statements can be backed up with other Scripture, we had best not assume the statements to be truth in the realm of doctrine. Many readers of the Bible have gone astray by taking some statements out of this book as truth to be believed, and the statements are out of harmony with the rest of the Bible. Remember this is man speaking his conclusion of what he has seen with his own eyes.

The final conclusion of the book in 12:13 can be taken two ways. Some take it as the complete answer of a Jew under the Law. This would be the answer in keeping with the Book of Proverbs. Others, however, say that this too must be taken with a grain of salt. The conclusion does not allow for the sin question and does not allow for the satisfaction of real life that a Jew found in faith in his God as seen in so many lives in the Old Testament.

The word *vanity* occurs 34 times; the expression "under the sun" occurs 29 times; the expression "upon the earth" is seen 7 times; and the phrase "under the heavens" is seen 3 times. These point out the nature of this book as a book that is a record of man's thinking apart from God.

To think your way through this book, it is necessary to follow the writer as he first shows that certain things that he has tried are really empty of any real lasting, complete satisfaction. Then the writer gives some advice in the light of these findings by showing what a man can do in this life of barrenness to make life at least a little more bearable.

Outline of the Book of Ecclesiastes

I   The theme stated   1:1–3
   A   The writer   1:1
   B   The theme   1:2–3

II   The theme proved   1:4–3:22
   A   By the cycle of life   1:4–11
   B   By the grief of wisdom   1:12–18
   C   By the emptiness of materialism   2:1–12
   D   By the law of inheritance   2:13–36
   E   By the surety of death   3:1–22

III   The theme expanded   4:1–12:8
   A   Inequalities of life   4
   B   Wealth   5

C   Man's end   6
D   Man's wickedness   7
E   God's providence   8–9
F   Disorders of life   10
G   Youth and old age   11:1–12:8

IV   Conclusion   12:8–14
A   The preacher   12:9–10
B   The words   12:11–12
C   The conclusion   12:13–14

SONG OF SOLOMON

In the Book of Song of Solomon we have the perfect picture of true love. This book so expresses true love that the Jews use it to express the love of God for Israel and the Christian uses it to express his love for God (and God's love for the saint).

The first verse shows that these experiences belong to that of Solomon. It is not fitting that such a book with such knowledge of intimate scenes in the love life of Solomon would be written by someone else. There is no good reason to doubt that Solomon was the author of this book just as he was of the two previous.

Since this book is the expression of two lovers, a word needs to be said concerning the purity of this book. Some have suggested that this book is obscene or even pornographic. According to definition, obscene is disgusting to the senses and designed to incite to lust or depravity. Pornography is defined as writing concerning harlots or, again, descriptions that are designed to excite. By these definitions this book is far from either. After reading this book one feels that true love is something very sacred.

There are some further considerations in the light of the subject matter of this book. It must be understood that the scenes of love in these pages are scenes between husband and wife. It must be remembered that the oriental often refers to parts of the body that we would blush to speak of with no

84

design of impurity or impropriety. Further, it must be remembered that the sexual life of a man is a valid area of his life and is pure if it is used correctly. The correct use of sex is stated in the Bible in clear terms. Hebrews 13:4 and 1 Corinthians 7:1–5 are both explicit in showing that sex in the marriage is normal and vital. The Bible is equally clear, however, that any sexual relations before marriage are sin no matter what the intentions are and no matter what the degree of love is between the parties. The reader is invited to read Matthew 5:27–28; Leviticus 18; and Revelation 21:8.

Some have suggested that the story of this book is the story of King Solomon trying to win the love of a young girl away from her true lover. The true lover is to be seen as the shepherd whom the girl loves and from whom Solomon tries to win her by his riches and ways. A better understanding seems to be that of Solomon and the girl without any third party. The shepherd lover is in reality Solomon who had disguised himself upon visiting his vineyards so he might obtain a true report of the business of the vineyards. The story unfolds when the girl falls in love with him as a shepherd and he falls in love with her. He has to continue on with his business, but he promises to return for her. He does not tell her, however, that he is really King Solomon.

While he is away, the girl dreams of him and eagerly awaits his return. She is greatly surprised when he does return in his chariot and with his mighty men to take her to his palace. The rest of the book is the story of love between these two with the book ending with the two lovers going back to her home for a second honeymoon.

It will be noted that this story is not a continued story through the book, but must be put together by seeing the various parts of the book. The vineyard is seen in 8:11, and the girl's relation to it is seen in chapter 1. Solomon is seen in chapter 1 as the lover who must leave but promises to return. Chapter 2 relates the thoughts of the two for each other and chapter 3 shows the return of Solomon for his promised bride. From chapter 4 on, the sections are statements of the love relation between these two.

The Song of Solomon is a book that should be read often. Young people would profit by seeing that God is concerned with this part of their life, and those who have been married for a number of years would also profit by seeing that love is constantly to be expressed to the mate. If more married couples would read this book, both together and separately, perhaps more marriages would be what God would have them be.

As a help in following the speaker, keep in mind that *beloved* is masculine, and *love* is feminine. Thus 1:9 must be Solomon speaking of her, and 1:16 must be the girl speaking of Solomon.

Rather than outlining this book, it may aid just as well to title each chapter.

Chapter Headings for the Song of Solomon

1 The Woman and the Shepherd
2 The Promise to Return
3 The Return
4 His Description of Her
5 A Dream She Had
6 Her Beauty Praised
7 Lover's Communion
8 The Return Back Home

6
Prophetic Books

ISAIAH

The Book of Isaiah is the first of the writing prophets in our English Bible, but it must be remembered that he is really about fifth in line by actual chronology. The reader is reminded that the best way to understand the prophets is to relate them to the Book of 2 Kings and to the exact time of their ministry. In most cases, it is possible to date the prophets by reading the first few verses of the book.

A possible chronological order of the prophets is Joel, Jonah, Amos, Hosea, Isaiah, Micah, Nahum, Zephaniah, Jeremiah, Habakkuk, Obadiah, Ezekiel, Daniel, Haggai, Zechariah, and Malachi. In this list, only Joel, Naham, Habakkuk, and Obadiah are not dated either in the book itself or in 2 Kings; so this listing is very close to being right with only a few variations possible.

In studying prophetical books one must remember that the prophets were the preachers of that time in Israel's history. Their main job was to get the nation to respond to Jehovah and to adjust their lives to His Law. As the captivities drew closer, it became more of an individual message rather than a national message since the nation was already judged. God was giving individual promises to those who would respond at that time.

Further, it is important that the reader of the prophets keep in mind that God cannot and will not cast off the nation of Israel. He will and does punish the nation for its sin, but He will still perform His promise that was made to Abraham, Isaac, and Jacob. Because of this fact, it is necessary to keep an eye open for prophecies concerning the future of Israel when God will cause them to enjoy all He has for them. Even in the face of the continued rebellion and disobedience as found in this period, God still maintains that His promise cannot fail. The themes and developments of the major and minor prophets are so much the same that one can almost predict what each book will say before he reads it. The only thing that will be different is the development of that theme or the variation of that theme, just as one will find in a great symphony.

According to Isaiah 1:1, the prophet had a ministry in the southern kingdom during the reigns of Uzziah, Jotham, Ahaz, and Hezekiah. This puts Isaiah in the time when Assyria was invading the land and when they took Israel (the northern tribes) into captivity. The time of Isaiah was a time of political unrest and fear, of political treaties, and of spiritual laxity, coupled with a time of revival under Hezekiah.

The name Isaiah means "Jehovah saves" or "salvation is of Jehovah." This is an apt description of the book, for God shows in this book that though He will judge, He will yet completely deliver or save the nation. This salvation is seen in a spiritual sense, in a contemporary sense, and in a future sense.

The Book of Isaiah reflects Isaiah in a very interesting way. This book shows that it was written by a man who was a real scholar. His vocabulary is the largest in any book of the Bible, and his style is a beauty to see in either Hebrew or English. Isaiah says things so well that we might wish we had said them.

The book has two main divisions, and they are easy to remember since the chapters correspond to the number of books in the Bible and to the two main divisions of the Bible. Chapters 1–39 form the first part. In this division the emphasis is on the judgment of the Lord, although this judgment is constantly related to the blessings that God has for the nation after this time of purging. Much of this section has to do with the present circumstance of the nation and much has to do with the future time of trouble coming on the nation and on the world, known as the tribulation. This tribulation period is to be followed by the Kingdom of God on the earth.

The second division is chapter 40 to the end of the book, chapter 66. This section emphasizes the greatness of Jehovah and the complete provisions He has made for the nation. The section begins with comfort, ends with glory, and just about in the middle is the way both of these can be man's, for chapter 53 shows us the Lamb of God who takes away our sin.

Isaiah has often been called the Old Testament Gospel since it has so much about Christ. The reader is encouraged to hunt for Christ as this book is read. Many important facts and features of His life and ministry can be found in this book.

Outline of the Book of Isaiah

The Emphasis on Judgment   1–39

    I Judgment that is followed by blessing   1–24
      A Judgment on Israel   1–12
      B Judgment on the nations   13–24

    II Blessing that is preceded by judgment   25–35
      A The process involved   25–27
      B The woes pronounced   28–33
      C The blessing realized   34–35

    III The historical example of deliverance   36–39
      A The present problem   36
      B The deliverance   37
      C The sickness and folly   38–39

Emphasis on Deliverance   40–66

    I Comfort from a great God   40–48
      A God and the idols   40–46
      B God and the nation   47–48

II Salvation from a great God 49–57
  A Promise of salvation 49–51
  B Person of salvation 52–53
  C Provisions of salvation 55–57

III Glory from a great God 58–66
  A The coming of glory 58–63
  B The establishment of glory 64–66

JEREMIAH

More is known about the prophet Jeremiah than any other prophet. His book is a reflection of himself and of his ministry. His name means "Jehovah forms or casts." He was a priest (1:1); he was chosen before his birth (1:5); he was told not to marry (16:1–4); he was hated and maltreated by his people; he was forced to go to Egypt after the fall of Jerusalem (chapter 43); and his heart was ever sensitive (9:1, and the Book of Lamentations).

Jeremiah prophesied from the reign of Josiah to the fall of Jerusalem. He was the last major voice before God gave His people into the hands of the Gentiles. Jeremiah's message is not one of possible deliverance of the nation from their present troubles, but it was one of promise to individuals that God would deliver and would establish the nation under the rule of David's Son and also that He would establish a new covenant with His people in that future day of blessing.

It was the Book of Jeremiah that Daniel was studying as recorded in Daniel 9:1–2, and it is this book that shows that the captivity of the nation would be for a period of seventy years.

The Book of Jeremiah can be considered in three parts. First, God speaks to the nation of Israel and shows their judgment and blessing. Then the Gentile nations are taken up and God pronounces His judgment on them. The last chapter is the third division and forms a vindication of all that has been said. Jeremiah early in his history had said Babylon would take the nation captive. Now he records this event to show that his words are the words of God. This shows to all who read this book that God's words are meant to be believed and to be understood. It is also a guide to interpretation since the things spoken of came to pass just as they were told.

Outline of the Book of Jeremiah

I   Words for Judah and Jerusalem   1–45
  A   The prophet and his call   1
  B   Eight messages of sin and repentance   2–20
  C   Messages of capitivity and blessing   21–39
  D   Messages to the remnant   40–45

II   Words for the nations   46–51
  A   Egypt   46
  B   Philistia   47
  C   Moab   48
  D   Ammon   49:1–6
  E   Edom   49:7–22
  F   Damascus   49:23–27
  G   Kedar and Hazor   49:28–33
  H   Elam   49:34–38
  I   Babylon   50:1–51:58

III   Words vindicated   52:1–34
  A   The capture of Jerusalem   52:1–11
  B   The destruction of Jerusalem   52:12–23
  C   The captives from Jerusalem   52:24–34

LAMENTATIONS

Tradition had consistently assigned the authorship of Lamentations to Jeremiah. This fact is graphically seen in the Septuagint version where these words are found as introductory:

> And it came to pass, after Israel had been carried away captive . . . that Jeremiah sat weeping and lamented with this lamentation . . . .

This book describes the conditions existing in Jerusalem as a result of the city's capture and burning by the Babylonian army. Some of the major features are: the young fainting (2:11, 12; 4:9); the city stormed (2:7; 4:12); the citizens carried away captive (1:5; 2:9); and the feasts, sabbaths, and Law no more (1:4; 2:6). Because of these events being a part of this book, it is no problem to assign it a date. These events took place in 586 B.C.

While this book is a lamentation over the fall of Jerusalem, it is, at the same time, a praise to the faithfulness of God. All that happened to the nation was a result of their sin; God was faithful and His mercies were ever new and fresh. The center verses of this book are the favorite 3:22–40, in which the greatnesses of God are extolled.

The structure of this book is interesting. The book is a poem (in the Hebrew sense) and is also an acrostic for the most part. The book consists of five separate poems corresponding to our chapters in the English. In the first, second, and fourth poems, each of the twenty-two stanzas begins with a letter of the Hebrew alphabet in proper order. In the third poem, the stanza contains three verses each beginning with the letter of that stanza, thus repeating each letter three times in the poem. The fifth poem does not follow the alphabetical arrangement, but it has twenty-two verses.

A summary can be given in terms of the subject matter of each poem.

Summary of the Book of Lamentations

1 The Solitude of a City Once So full
2 The Destruction of the City Once So Strong
3 The Prophet's Own Grief
4 The Suffering of the City Once So Rich
5 The Remembrance of the City Once So Blessed

EZEKIEL

Like Jeremiah, Ezekiel belongs to the priest family. Like Daniel, Ezekiel ministered and wrote from Babylon. Daniel was not exactly a preaching prophet while Ezekiel was. Both of these men were in Babylon, but Ezekiel had more of a ministry to his people while David remained the "friend in court" for the nation. Unlike Jeremiah, Ezekiel was married, yet he lost his wife (24:15-19).

Ezekiel's book is very well dated. He began his ministry in the fifth year of Jehoiachin's captivity (1:2), and continued until the twenty-seventh year (29:17). This means that Ezekiel's work was from 592 B.C. until 570 B.C. Throughout his book he gives the dates for the various messages so that the dates are easy to find.

While Ezekiel speaks of the normal things for a prophet and while he shows the future blessing for the nation as well as judgment for Israel and the nations, his particular emphasis seems to be twofold. The expression "that all may know that I am God" or its equivalent occurs sixty-two times in this book. Another prominent idea is the glory of God. The glory is seen in 1:28; 8:4; 9:3; 10:4, 18, 19; 11:22, 23; 43:2-5; and 44:4. Thus, this book develops these two great themes.

The method of Ezekiel is very up-to-date. Today teachers are constantly reminded to make their material graphic in every form possible. Ezekiel uses symbols, parables, dramatics, and anything that will get his point across better.

A word of caution might be good at this point. The fact that there are many symbols and such in this book does not mean that the events and prophecies are not literal or real. A look at history will show that the things spoken of by Ezekiel (like the other prophets) have come to pass with alarming accuracy (the prophecies regarding Tyre and Egypt are cases in point; see chapters 26-32).

From chapters 33 to the end of the book are some of the most pointed prophecies concerning the nation of Israel that can be found anywhere. In chapters 33-39 the restoration of the nation is graphically put before the reader. In chapters 40-48 there is a detailed account of the worship of Israel in the Kingdom and the place of Israel in the land.

Outline of the Book of Ezekiel

    I   The call of Ezekiel   1-3
        A   A vision for the work   1
        B   A call to the work   2-3

II The prophecies against Israel 4–24
  A Four signs of judgment 4–7
  B Four visions of judgment 8–11
  C Parables and messages of judgment 12–19
  D Jerusalem and judgment 20–24

III The prophecies against the nations 25-32
  A Ammon 25:1–7
  B Moab 25:8–11
  C Edom 25:12–14
  D Philistia 25:15–17
  E Tyre 26–28:19
  F Sidon 28:20–26
  G Egypt 29–32

IV The prophecies of restoration 33–39
  A The watchman 33
  B The shepherds 34
  C The sequence 35:1–36:7
  D The restoration prophesied 36:8–38
  E The restoration illustrated 37
  F The battle 38–39

V The prophecies of Kingdom features 40–48
  A The temple 40–43:12
  B The worship 43:13–46:24
  C The land 47–48

DANIEL

To this "man greatly beloved" (9:23; 10:11, 19) was given some of the most detailed and far-reaching prophecies of the Word of God. The four great world powers of Gentile dominion, the coming of the time of trouble upon the earth, the coming of a man to head up the last world power before the coming of Christ, the coming of Christ and the establishment of the Kingdom, the time of the seventy weeks of Israel that sets the stage for the time period of the great tribulation (time of trouble coming upon the world), and the resurrection of the righteous of the nation of Israel, are some of the major revelations of this book.

Not only is the Book of Daniel of great interest to all Bible students, but Daniel is also a man to be studied. His life was marked by constant prayer (chapters 2, 6, 9, 10); he was guided by a study of God's Word (9:1–2; he had a testimony of life (chapter 6) and lip (chapters 2, 4, 5); and he was dedicated to keeping himself pure for God (1:8). Truly this man is worthy of study.

The Book of Daniel presents that time when Jerusalem was under control of Gentiles and when Israel was not in its place before God. Daniel shows that this time started in the third year of the reign of Jehoiachin. It was marked by the rise and fall of four great Gentile powers. Three of these great world powers are named as Babylon, Media-Persia, and Greece; the fourth is implied strongly as the power that follows Greece, which was Rome. This period will come to a close after the last world power has a man over it that is totally against God and against the people of Israel. This one is destroyed by God Himself and God's Kingdom will be established on the earth, never to be given to another people.

The Book of Daniel is usually divided into two main sections, the first being events and experiences that show the times of the Gentiles and the second being prophecies or visions given to Daniel showing this same period.

Outline of the Book of Daniel

I   Experiences and the time   1–6
   A   The beginning   1
   B   The dream of the image   2
   C   The furnace   3
   D   The dream of the tree   4
   E   The feast of Beltshazzar   5
   F   The lion's den   6

II   Visions and the time   7–12
   A   The four beasts   7

B The two beasts 8
C The seventy weeks 9
D The last days 10–12

HOSEA

The home life of Hosea forms a basis for the book that bears his name. God uses the events in the life of His prophet to speak of the relationship between Him and His people. This is another of the Old Testament books which shows that God cannot cast off or forget His nation Israel.

Hosea married a woman named Gomer, who, according to God's Word, was going to be a harlot. This marriage is used by God to speak of His uniting with the nation of Israel and her subsequent turning from Him to others. To the marriage were born three children. Jezreel, which means "scattered or planted by God," was the first. Then the second child was named Lo-ruhamah, which means "no mercy or not pitied." The third child was called Lo-ammi, which means "not my people or no kin of mine." These three children are used to represent the relation of individuals to God or the relation of the nation to God at various times. There is coming a time when the nation will be scattered from Jerusalem, and at this time Israel will be considered not pitied and not God's children. But a time is coming when He will plant them in their land and then they will be pitied and they will be His people (2:23).

The story of the home life of Hosea with his love for Gomer and the analogy between these events and Israel is found in the first three chapters. After chapter 3, Hosea continues by showing the sins of Israel and God's salvation (Hosea's name means "Jehovah saves"). Hosea ministered at the same time as Isaiah (1:1) and is considered by some to be one of the longest ministering prophets. From his constant reference to the northern tribe of Ephraim and by the fact that he refers to the king of the north as his king (7:3–5), it appears that Hosea was in the north.

The particular theme of Hosea is God's love for His adulterous nation.

Outline of the Book of Hosea

I   The adulterous wife   1–3
   A   The marriage and home   1
   B   The marriage applied   2
   C   The adulteress brought back   3

II   The adulterous nation   4–14
   A   The record established   4–5
   B   The response of Jehovah   6–9
   C   The remembrance of the past   10–11
   D   The recompense to the nation   12–13:8
   E   The restoration to favor   13:9–14:9

JOEL

The Book of Joel has no date in the book itself. This has caused a minor problem in that many do not know in which period to place it. Some authorities have placed the book very late in Israel's history while others have placed it very early. A possible solution is found by noting certain things in the book. To begin with, there is no mention of the Assyrian invasion of the land and, if it were written after this event, the nation of Assyria would certainly be mentioned as subject to judgment for their treatment of Israel. This appears relevant since other nations do receive condemnation for their acts toward the Israelites (3:2–8). This suggests that the book ought to be placed before 790 B.C., when Assyria first started oppressing Israel.

In the Book of Joel the reader will notice that no king is mentioned. There was a time in the nation's history, however, that would fit this circumstance. The key figures in the book are the priests. There was a time when the priests were in charge of the nation since there was a queen (Athaliah) running the affairs of state. After she was removed, the priests still continued to hold the reins of government since the new king was a child (compare with 2 Kings 11–12). It is therefore possible that the book was written during this time and would become the first book written by a prophet (about 830 B.C.).

The Book of Joel is a prophetic picture of the judgment and blessing of the future, built around a locust plague that was present at the time Joel wrote. It is obvious that the events spoken of (2:20–32; 3:1–8; 3:17–21) have not come to pass, so the main portion of this book awaits a future time for fulfillment.

Peter used a part of this book when he preached on the day of Pentecost. But from a study of both passages it does not look like he was saying the things were being fulfilled (compare Joel 2:28–32 and Acts 2:17–21). Rather, it seems that Peter was using this prophecy to show that the events of Pentecost were Spirit events and not events that should be attributed to wine. The real fulfillment of these things is still in the future.

Outline of the Book of Joel

I   The locust plague   1
   A   The extent of the plague   1:1–4
   B   The result upon the land   1:5–13
   C   The response of the priests   1:14–15
   D   The result upon the animals   1:16–20

II   The prophetic counterpart   2–3
   A   The invasion of the land   2:1–12
   B   The repentance of the people   2:13–17
   C   The deliverance by Jehovah   2:18–32
   D   The judgment upon the nations   3:1–16
   E   The blessing of the Kingdom   3:17–21

AMOS

The date for Amos is given three ways in the book. He says in the first verse that this message came in the days of Uzziah, in the days of Jeroboam II, and two years before the great earthquake (compare Zechariah 14:15). This would put his book sometime between 787 B.C. and 749 B.C.

Amos himself was a man of the south (1:1) for Tekoa was a place just south of Jerusalem, but his ministry was chiefly in the north. Further, Amos was not one of the professional prophets. He shows this in 7:14 when he claims he is not of the prophet line. He completes the picture of himself by calling himself two things. He is a herdsman and a gatherer of the sycamore fruit. The latter title is most interesting since the word for gatherer and the custom of the day was for the gatherer to pinch the fruit to make it ripen. This is most fitting, for Amos did indeed pinch the nation to help make it ripe and profitable to God. He also tried to bring the wandering sheep back to the fold as a true herdsman.

This untrained preacher develops his book in a most fascinating manner. First, he pronounces judgment upon all who have sinned, beginning with the Gentile nations and working up to the two divisions of the nation of Israel. This he does by starting far away from Israel and working in closer to her. (Follow his messages on a map and see his manner.) After showing that Israel is in line for judgment, he proceeds to pinpoint the sins of the nation that have made this necessary. True to the general theme of the prophets, he does not leave us or the nation with the question whether God is through with them. In the last section, he shows that God will ultimately bless this nation through the establishment of the Kingdom that was promised to David.

Amos is interesting in that he is probably the last prophetic voice the north had that was exclusive to them before their captivity. It is no wonder God had to take them into captivity when we see the result of his preaching was a request for him to go back home and do his preaching in the south (7:10–13).

Outline of the Book of Amos

 I The judgment upon the transgressors 1:1–2:16
  A Damascus 1:1–5

B   Gaza   1:6–8
C   Tyrus   1:9–10
D   Edom   1:11–12
E   Ammon   1:13–15
F   Moab   2:1–3
G   Judah   2:4–5
H   Israel   2:6–16

II   The sins of the transgressors   3:1–6:14
A   Misused privileges   3:1–15
B   Misguided worship   4:1–5
C   Misinterpreted warnings   4:6–13
D   Lamentation for Israel   5:1–27
E   Woe for Israel   6:1–14

III   The warnings to transgressors   7:1–9:10
A   Grasshopper plague   7:1–3
B   Fire   7:4–6
C   Plumb line   7:7–9
D   Amaziah   7:10–17
E   Summer fruit   8:1–14
F   Lintel   9:1–10

IV   The establishment of the Kingdom   9:11–15
A   The government   9:11
B   The people   9:12
C   The blessing   9:13
D   The peace   9:14
E   The duration   9:15

OBADIAH

Nothing is known of the man who wrote this book. His name means "servant of God," and as such he does not think that knowledge of himself is important. He has a master to represent, and this is the important feature.

The date of this book depends upon the plundering of Jerusalem by the Edomites (11–14). There are four recorded plunderings: in the reign of Jehoram (2 Chronicles 21:80), in the reign of Amaziah (2 Chronicles 25:11), in the reign of Ahaz (2 Chronicles 28:16), and in the reign of Zedekiah (2 Chronicles 36:11). It seems best to date this book after all of these, thus making it a judgment based on a complete story. This would place the book somewhere around 600 B.C.

The main idea of this book is to show the judgment upon the nation of Edom. This book has been graphically fulfilled as any history book will show. The city where the Edomites dwelt in the clefts of the rocks is the famed Petra of Edom.

Even though the main idea of the book is judgment, also included is the idea of blessing. In the last section of the book (it is only one chapter), there is the promise of the deliverance for the nation of Israel and the final possessing of their possessions (the land and Kingdom of the covenants).

Outline of the Book of Obadiah

I   Judgment announced   1–9
II   Judgment defended   10–14
III   Jerusalem established   15–21

JONAH

Jonah was a prophet of the middle 800's in the northern kingdom. He is mentioned in 2 Kings 14:23–27, and the content of his ministry is summed up in these few verses. He spoke of the establishment of the northern tribes and of the fact that they would not be blotted out.

As further confirmation that this man lived and prophesied, the Lord Jesus also referred to him and He called him a prophet (Matthew 12:39–41). Not only did Jesus affirm his office, but He affirmed that fact of his experience in the fish. Christ even used the time period of Jonah's experience as a symbol of His experience in the tomb.

The prophet Jonah was from the city of Gath-hepher, which is a city in the southern end of Galilee. This is especially interesting since the leaders of Israel at the time of Christ had forgotten this fact when they said that no prophet came from Galilee (John 7:52).

The story of this book is probably familiar to most Bible readers. God told Jonah to go announce judgment upon Nineveh (1:1; 3:1–4). Jonah did not want to go since he figured if he went Nineveh would repent and God would not judge them (4:1–2). This fact of the harshness of the prophet should be seen in the light of the fact that Assyria was Israel's enemy, and Jonah was a very nationalistic prophet (2 Kings 14). God in His greatness put Jonah through the experience of being swallowed by the great fish so that he would come to the place of doing what God wanted him to do (1:17–2:10), Jonah went to Nineveh, preached, and saw the city turn to God (3:5–10). The book ends with Jonah having a controversy with God about His mercy and with God dealing in mercy with a troubled prophet.

The reader is encouraged to trace certain ideas through the book. Notice: (1) the things that God prepared; (2) the downward journey that Jonah made in not doing God's will; and (3) the complete sovereignty of God in all realms.

Outline of the Book of Jonah

    I   Jonah fleeing   1

             Jonah goes west when he was told to go east, and he ends up down.

   II   Jonah praying   2

             From the stomach of the great fish, Jonah comes to his senses and promises to do God's will.

  III   Jonah preaching   3

             With his new commission, Jonah goes to the city of Nineveh and preaches, and the city repents.

  IV   Jonah pouting   4

             An angry prophet sits down on the outside of the city and God gives him an object lesson.

MICAH

The name Micah means "who is like Jehovah," and the book that bears this title is a treatise on the subject that there is no God like Jehovah. This book is an excellent one to see the character and acts of Jehovah in relation to the nation of Israel.

Micah was prophesying at the same time as Isaiah and Hosea. In 1:1, he tells us that he ministered in the days of Jotham, Ahaz, and Hezekiah. His book is addressed to both kingdoms, though he probably spent his time in the south since the kings mentioned are southern kings.

The fact that Micah and Isaiah were contemporaries can be seen by noting that their vocabularies are similar and by noting that in many places their expressions are the same. This does not in any way lessen the view of inspiration that one holds. It is still true that God worked in the hearts and minds of the writers so that the very words that He wanted them to write were written, but it is also true that He did so in such a way as to preserve the identity of the writer. It is a common thing in the realm of literature for one man to be influenced by the writing of another; so the fact that Isaiah and Micah have things in common does not lessen our view of the men or of inspiration.

The Book of Micah can be studied or understood by noting three sections of the book. First, Micah shows that there is no God like Jehovah in His *judgment*. After this section he shows that there is no God like Jehovah in His *deliverance*. Finally he shows that there is no God like Jehovah in his *righteousness*. It is this last section then that forms the basis of the other two. Because God is righteous, He must punish sin; this is seen in the first section. God has also made certain promises to Israel and, if He is righteous, He must perform them. Thus, the second section.

Chapter 7:7–9 presents one of the best unfoldings of salvation as an Old Testament saint viewed it. In these verses we see that man is a sinner and must bear his judgment. This is further developed to show that God Himself will plead for the

103

sinner, and that the righteousness of God is at stake and provided. All of this is made available to the sinner by a personal relation to Jehovah (note the personal pronouns in this section). Thus, it can be seen that a personal relation with the God of righteousness will provide, through the intervention of God Himself, a salvation for the sinner.

In chapters 4 and 5 we also see one of the best descriptions of the Kingdom that God will establish with the nation of Israel. The king and his birthplace are set forth in chapter 5, and the essentials of the Kingdom are set forth in chapter 4. The reader is invited to study these passages and note the things said.

Outline of the Book of Micah

I   The incomparable God of judgment   1–3
   A   Announcement of judgment   1:1–7
   B   Cites and Judgment   1:8–16
   C   Indictment for judgment   2:1–11
   D   Administration of judgment   2:12–13
   E   Denouncement of judgment   3:1–12

II   The incomparable God of deliverance   4–5
   A   Blessing in deliverance   4:1–8
   B   Need for deliverance   4:9–5:1
   C   Person of deliverance   5:2–9
   D   Execution of deliverance   5:10–15

III   The incomparable God of righteousness   6–7
   A   Repentance based on God's righteousness   6:1–8
   B   Judgment according to God's righteousness   6:9–16
   C   Antithesis to God's righteousness   7:1–6
   D   The God of righteousness   7:7–20

NAHUM

The theme and development of Nahum is easy to find and to follow. This book deals with the judgment upon the city of Nineveh just as Obadiah deals with the judgment upon Edom.

The development is simply the stating of judgment and then the description of judgment along with the cause for it.

Nahum is another of the books of the Old Testament that can be read with a history book in mind since the things spoken of in this book have been graphically fulfilled. This book speaks of the overthrow of the city of Nineveh, with a great spoiling of the city and with the waters of the city becoming its enemy. All of this was done when Babylon finally took the city in the year 612 B.C.

There is no date in the book itself. Some readers of the Bible who do not want to admit such a thing as the supernatural and prophecy have to assign a date after the fall of Nineveh. Most readers of the Bible, however are not afraid to say that this book was written before the events took place and this becomes just another proof of the uniqueness of this book, the Bible. Since no king is mentioned in the book, and since this book deals with the overthrow of the city that was responsible for the captivity of the northern tribes, it might be best to date it somewhere near the fall of Samaria to the Assyrians. There would be no king of the north to mention, and this book would be a comfort to those of Israel that were questioning God's actions. An accepted date would probably be 700 B.C.

This is the second book in the Bible that has Nineveh as a major subject. Jonah was sent to this city about one hundred fifty years earlier, and the people turned to God. God waited these years to pronounce His final judgment upon the city. The turning to God at the preaching of Jonah was not a lasting or complete turning. There was only one thing God could do, and He foretells this in the Book of Nahum.

Outline of the Book of Nahum

    I Overthrow foretold 1
        A The God who judges 1:1–7
        B The judgment of God 1:8–15

   II Overthrow described 2
        A The city taken 2:1–8
        B The city spoiled 2:9–13

III   Overthrow deserved   3
    A   City of bloodshed   3:1–3
    B   City of idolatry   3:4–7
    C   City of pride   3:8–19

HABAKKUK

The key verse of the Book of Habakkuk (2:4) is quoted three times in the New Testament—Romans 1:17, Galatians 3:11, and Hebrews 10:38. Each of these New Testament books is a key book in the development of faith, and Habakkuk is a key book in this sense in the Old Testament.

The prophet Habakkuk had a problem. He could not understand why God was not judging the nation of Judah for her sin (1:1–4). God answers this problem by telling Habakkuk that He will judge Judah and that He will use Babylon to do it (1:5–11). This only causes the prophet to have a greater problem, for this would mean that God was using a sinful nation to punish his own people, and God is too righteous to do this (1:12–2:1). Jehovah's answer to this problem is twofold. His primary answer is the key to the book. Man is to live by faith in God, that is, man is to trust God to do that which is right. The second part of the answer is to show that God will also punish Babylon (2:2–20).

Habakkuk learned his lesson well. The final chapter of his book is a psalm that centers in God. The final verses of the chapter show that now the prophet is centered on God; no matter what happens around him, he can rest in Jehovah.

This book, another of the undated ones, can probably be put in the reign of Josiah since Babylon was just beginning to come into prominence at that time.

Outline of the Book of Habakkuk

I   The dialogue   1:1–2:20
    A   The first round   1:1–11
    B   The second round   1:12–2:20

II The doxology 3
   A The person of God 3:1–15
   B The praise of the prophet 3:16–19

ZEPHANIAH

The prophet Zephaniah gives to us the best lineage of any of the prophets. Some have suggested that the Hezekiah of the first verse might well be King Hezekiah, and this would of course make Zephaniah of royal descent. This may or may not be the case. But we can be sure that all knew this man by the exact genealogy he gave.

Zephaniah wrote in the reign of Josiah, in the last years of the southern kingdom. The prophet Jeremiah was also active in this general period.

The theme of this book is the Day of the Lord. This phrase is one that occurs many times in the prophets, and it can be understood in two main ways. It often refers to a present time of judgment such as the locust plague of Joel or the impending invasion of the land by Assyria or Babylon. It also may be speaking of the time in the future when God will deal in judgment and blessing. This future time is also called the tribulation and the Kingdom. The awesome description that appears in this book makes it necessary to conclude that it is referring in the main to the time in the future. It is no wonder that the period of judgment is spoken of as a period that has no equal (Daniel 12:1; Matthew 24:21).

Outline of the Book of Zephaniah

  I Troubles in the Day of the Lord 1:1–3:7
    A Judah in that day 1:1–2:3
    B Nations in that day 2:4–15
    C God and that day 3:1–7

 II Blessings in the Day of the Lord 3:8–20
    A The remnant 3:8–13

107

B   The king   3:14–17
C   The regathering   3:18–20

HAGGAI

The Book of Haggai is of the period of Ezra and Nehemiah. The last three prophets of the Old Testament are often called the post-exilic prophets. These three books center in the nation and their actions upon their return to the land after the Babylonian captivity.

The date of Haggai is given as the second year of the reign of Darius. This would be 520 B.C., sixteen years after the end of the seventy years of captivity. It will be remembered that the nation was allowed to return to their homeland in 536 B.C.

According to Ezra 5:1 and 6:14, Haggai and the prophet Zechariah encouraged the people in the work of rebuilding the temple. The people had allowed enemies to stop their work on the temple. In the meantime, the people had built their own homes and were not bothering with the work of God. This book is the record of how God worked through the prophet to get the people to restart and to finish the work of building the temple.

The Book of Haggai is a record of five messages of the prophet that were delivered at different times. Each message is recorded with its proper date and these five messages are the easiest way to think through this book.

Outline of the Book of Haggai

1   Message of rebuke   1:1–11
2   Message of promise   1:12–15
3   Message of encouragement   2:1–9
4   Message of cleansing   2:10–19
5   Message of establishment   2:20–23

ZECHARIAH

At the same time Haggai was speaking to the people about their relation to the work of the temple, Zechariah was speaking to them concerning their relation to God and to His promises. The Book of Zechariah is a book of encouragement to Israel that God will yet bring peace and prosperity to Jerusalem. This blessing will come through future trouble, but it will come.

The coming of Christ to Jerusalem in His first coming is described in this book in the famed passage of His riding on the donkey into the city (9:9). Also in this book is one of the most graphic pictures of the return of Christ to Jerusalem where He is seen as touching the Mount of Olives (14:4). Just as Isaiah can be called the Messianic major prophet, one might well call Zechariah the Messianic minor prophet.

The prophet's name means "the Lord remembers," and this is seen throughout the book. God has not, nor will He ever, forget His people. They may be scattered throughout the world, but they are still the "apple of his eye" (2:8), and He will yet bring to pass all His promises to this nation. This nation will possess Jerusalem, they will have Christ as king, and they will be the favored nation of the world. All these prophesies have not come to pass yet; but God keeps His word, and we can look for these great events in the future.

Outline of the Book of Zechariah

I   The eight visions 1:1–6:15 Israel's pictorial history
   A   The rider among the myrtle trees   1:1–17
   B   The horns and smiths   1:18–21
   C   The man with the measuring line   2:1–13
   D   The cleansing of Joshua   3:1–10
   E   The candlestick   4:1–14
   F   The flying roll   5:1–4
   G   The ephah   5:5–11
   H   The four chariots   6:1–8
   I   The consuming action   6:9–15

II   The four messages 7:1–8:23 Israel's questions
   A   Message of exhortation   7:1–7
   B   Message of explanation   7:8–14
   C   Message of expectation   8:1–17
   D   Message of exaltation   8:18–23

III The two burdens 9:1–14:21 Israel's future
    A Burden upon the nations 9–11
    B Burden upon the nation 12–14

MALACHI

The last book in our English Old Testament is the Book of Malachi. Although Malachi is the last of the prophets of the Old Testament, it is very possible that the book is not the last one written in the Old Testament period. Many place the book in the period of Nehemiah while there was a "governor" (1:8), and while the people were still far from God in their actions (perhaps between the first and second reforms of Nehemiah).

This is the final message from God to a rebellious people, and shows how bad the people still were after the captivity. The nation of Israel was not in proper relationship with the God of Abraham, Isaac, and Jacob. Thus, the Old Testament is seen to end on an incomplete note. The promises of God to the nation have not come to pass and the promise of the Redeemer has not been fulfilled. But the book does end with a bright hope. God is yet going to visit His people and establish His promises (4:1–6).

The Book of Malachi revolves around certain statements by God and the resultant questions of the people. This is seen by the repeated phrase, "but ye say, Wherein . . ." (1:2; 1:6; 1:7; 2:17; 3:7; 3:8; 3:13). An understanding of these statements and questions will make it easy to follow this book.

Outline of the Book of Malachi

    1 Statement of God's love 1:1–5
    2 Statement of people despising God 1:6–2:9
    3 Statement of laxed law 2:10–16
    4 Statement of promised judgment 2:17–3:6
    5 Statement of robbing God 3:7–12
    6 Statement of future blessing 3:13–4:6

7

New Testament History

MATTHEW

The New Testament opens with four books that present the life of Christ in four different ways or ideas. These four books are called the Gospels because they tell the "good news" that God has come to die for man in order that man can live with God. Just as Genesis is the only book that can rightly start the Old Testament, these are the only books that can start the New Testament. Further, of the four, Matthew is perhaps the best one to be the bridge between the Old and the New.

Matthew presents Jesus in the light of the fulfilment of the Old Testament promises for the Redeemer and the King of Israel. Mark shows the life of Christ in the role of a servant. Luke brings the humanity of Jesus to the fore, while John sees to it that the deity of Christ is not overlooked. Each of these is important but as the book to form the link between the two testaments, Matthew fits best.

These four representations of Jesus are not without cause. The Old Testament had pictured Him in just such a manner. In Zechariah 9:9 and Jeremiah 23:5, the King is seen. Isaiah 42:1 and Zechariah 3:8 show the servant. The humanity is seen in Zechariah 6:12, and the deity presents itself in Isaiah 40:9 and Isaiah 4:2. These are not the only passages that relate to these ideas, but there is a parallel that can be seen in each of these.

Matthew, Mark, and Luke are called the synoptic Gospels. This means that they view Christ's life from somewhat the same viewpoint. John's Gospel is so different in its content that it must be set apart. This does not mean that the three books are in disagreement or opposition to John. There was so much in Christ's life that the world might not be able to contain all the books and material that could be written (John 21:25). These four books therefore are just a sampling of what He did and said.

Matthew was one of Jesus' disciples. As such, he traveled with Him, and this is a firsthand report of the things recorded. Of the synoptic writers, he is unique in this aspect. We further know that this man was a collector of taxes or customs before Christ called him to follow Him.

The key to an understanding of this book is to follow the unfolding of the Kingdom program through the book. Matthew is showing to any who would want to know (the Jew particularly) that the Messiah had indeed come; He had promised to establish the Kingdom of the Old Testament; He was rejected; and because of this He set the nation of Israel aside and proclaims the promise of the Church. However, there will be a fulfilling of the Kingdom promises at a time in the future. Of the three synoptic writers, Matthew perhaps pays the least attention to chronology. He is developing a theme rather than showing a systematic life of Christ. This does not mean to say that the chronology of Christ's life is completely overlooked, for the main outline of the book is chronological. But the events in each section are not necessarily put in their proper order since that is not the purpose.

Outline of the Gospel of Matthew

I   The offer of the Kingdom   1–10
   A   The rights of the King   1–4
   B   The preaching of the King   5–7
   C   The authority of the King   8–10

II   The rejection of the Kingdom   11–23
   A   Declaration of the rejection   11–12
   B   Consequence of the rejection   13
   C   Unfolding of the rejection   14–22:14
   D   The double rejection   22:15–23:39

112

III The promise of the Kingdom 24–25
    A The circumstance 24:1–3
    B The teachings 24:4–31
    C The parables 24:32–25:46

IV The transition from the Kingdom 26–28
    A Crucifixion of the King 26–27
    B Resurrection of the King 28:1–15
    C Commission of the King 28:16–20

MARK

Tradition has long said that Mark wrote through the eyes of Peter. It is considered true that Mark and Peter were the ones responsible for this book, and most maintain that this book is the first of the gospels. It is interesting to note that the Book of Mark is an expansion of Peter's sermon to Cornelius, as seen in Acts 10:34–43.

The Book of Mark with its emphasis on Christ as a servant does not have a genealogy as Matthew does. It is important that the King's rights be established by a correct genealogy, but a genealogy does not matter in regard to a servant. The essential feature of a servant is that he can perform. The key word in Mark, therefore, is the word *straightway,* which means *then next* or *immediately.* It is a word of action. This action and activity is furthered by seeing the many miracles recorded in this, the shortest of the gospels, and by seeing that twice this book records that the disciples did not have leisure time to eat (3:20; 6:31).

The action of this book does not take away from the words of the servant. His sayings are set forth in very concise terms and then the actions are seen as vindications of His words.

Chapter 10, verse 45, can be made to be a key to the book. This verse shows that there are two broad divisions to the life of Christ. First, He comes to serve and then He comes to give His life. This division can be recognized in the Book of Mark by 1:1–8:26 and by 8:27–16:20. It is interesting to see that each section then begins with a declaration of who Christ is, with an anointing, and with a temptation or test. Without forcing the outline, it can be seen that Mark is following a plan or order in his presentation of Christ's life. The order is in the selection of material and not in a change of chronology, thus leaving the Gospel of Mark as the book of chronology of Christ's life.

Outline of the Gospel of Mark

    I   Coming to serve   1:11–8:26
        A   First Galilean ministry   1:1–3:35
            1   Teachings and miracles   1:1–2:12
            2   Questions and rejections   2:13–3:12
            3   Christ and His disciples   3:13–19
            4   Pharisees   3:20–35

        B   Second Galilean ministry   4:1–8:26
            1   Teachings and miracles   4:1–5:43
            2   Questions and rejections   6.1–6
            3   Christ and His disciples   6:7–56
            4   Pharisees   7:1–8:26

   II   Coming to die   8:27–16:20
        A   His last teachings   8:27–13:37
            1   Regarding His person   8:27–9:32
            2   Regarding His life values   9:33–10:52
            3   Regarding His rejection and authority
                                      11:1–12:44
            4   Regarding His return   13:1–37

        B   His last days   14:1–16:20
            1   The preparation   14:1–42
            2   The trials   14:43–15:15
            3   The crucifixion   15:16–47
            4   The resurrection and ascension   16:1–20

LUKE

Luke is one of the interesting men of the New Testament. He is mentioned or seen in Acts 16:1–17; 20:4–15; 21:1–18;

27:1–28; Colossians 4:14; Philemon 24; and 2 Timothy 4:11. In these passages it can be seen that he is a Gentile, a physician, a well-educated man, a companion of Paul, and a man called of God. The veracity of facts listed in his two books (Luke and Acts) have often been attacked, but they have also more often been proven. This man, who was a physician, a missionary, and a writer, was also a historian of excellent quality.

This Gospel is one book of a set, since both Acts and Luke are addressed to the same individual (Theophilus) and one is the continuation of the other. Luke began his writings by a careful investigation of all the facts (Luke 1:1–4); then he very carefully wrote the account of Christ's life. The main purpose of the Gospel of Luke seems to be to show that Christ was indeed a Man among men. To the Greek mind, the humanity of Jesus would be important, and this book brings this out. The development of this theme is done in such a way as to keep the deity of Jesus also before the reader.

Three easy ways to show the main thrust of the book are: (1) to see that the genealogy is traced all the way back to Adam; (2) to note the constant use of the phrase "son of man"; and (3) to observe the human qualities stressed such as prayer, feelings, etc.

Outline of the Gospel of Luke

    I   Birth and childhood of the Man   1–3
        A   Birth and growth of John   1
        B   Birth and growth of Jesus   2
        C   Baptism of Jesus by John   3

   II   Temptation of the Man   4:1–13
        A   The first trial   4.1–4
        B   The second trial   4:5–8
        C   The third trial   4:9–13

  III   Ministry of the Man   4:14 19:28
        A   Ministry in Galilee   4:14–9:50
        B   Ministry on the way to Jerusalem   9:51–19:28

IV Death of the Man   19:29–23:56
   A   His entry to the city   19:28–46
   B   His teaching in the temple   19:47–21:38
   C   His last night with the disciples   22:1–46
   D   His death for the world   22:47–23:56

 V Resurrection of the Man   24:1–53
   A   The fact   24:1–12
   B   The fellowship   24:13–35
   C   The disciples   24:36–49
   D   The ascension   24:50–53

JOHN

The other gospel written by a disciple of Jesus is the Gospel of John. This is one of five books written by John for he also wrote three epistles and The Revelation. Of all the gospel writers, John is the only one that explicitly states the purpose of his book. In 20:31 he says that he has written his book to show the deity of Jesus and the importance of believing on Him.

Of all the Gospels, John's is perhaps the most read. John presents the incidents of Christ's life in simple terms that all can enjoy; yet, he has the ability in the very same words to show the greatness of the theology of the New Testament. As one reads these words of John, one is sure that Jesus is God and is living today.

There are some unique things about this Gospel so that it cannot be called a synoptic Gospel. There are some unique discourses: the New Birth, chapter 3; the Water of Life, chapter 4; the Bread of Life, chapter 6; the Light of the World, chapter 8; the Good Shepherd, chapter 10; and the Upper Room, chapters 13 to 17. At the same time there are some unique absences. The Olivet discourse, scribes, lepers, publicans, demoniacs, and parables are absent. John's Gospel is indeed different.

John tells us that he is selecting certain "signs" that Jesus did and building his Gospel around them (20:31). These signs

116

are easy to find and to follow: (1) water to wine, chapter 2; (2) nobleman's son, chapter 4; (3) man at the pool, chapter 5; (4) feeding the 5,000, chapter 6; (5) walking on the water, chapter 6; (6) blind man, chapter 9; (7) Lazarus, chapter 11; (8) the fish, chapter 21. By following these signs and the statements about them we come to the conclusion that this One is indeed God.

There are seven great sayings of Christ in the Gospel of John that have the phrase "I am" in them, and they are certainly worth noting. They are: "the bread of life" (6:35); "the light of the world (8:12); "the door" (10:7); "the good shepherd" (10:11); "the resurrection" (11:25); the "way" (14:6); and "the vine" (15:5).

Certainly one of the great sections of John's Gospel is the section known as the "Upper Room Discourse." This discourse is found in chapters 13–17 and gives to us some of the most precious truths. The reader should become familiar with this section. The prayer of Christ as recorded in chapter 17 is indeed a "holy ground experience."

Outline of the Gospel of John

I   Christ and the world   1:1–12:50
   A   Who is Christ   1
   B   His testimony to individuals   2–5
   C   His testimony to groups   6–10
   D   How He was received   11–12

II   Christ and the disciples   13–17
   A   The example to follow   13
   B   The comforter to come   14
   C   The relationship to enjoy   15
   D   The truth to believe   16
   E   The prayer to ponder   17

III   Christ and the cross   18–19
   A   In the garden   18:1–11
   B   In the courtroom   18:12–27
   C   In Pilate's hall   18:28–19:15
   D   On the cross   19:16–37

IV Christ and the resurrection 19:38–21:25
  A Placed in the tomb 19:38–42
  B Raised from the dead 20:1–10
  C Seen after the resurrection 20:11–31
  D Instructions before the ascension 21:1–25

ACTS

The second book written by Luke is the Book of Acts. In chapter one, verse one, he explains the relation of this book to the Gospel of Luke and also shows what he is doing in this book. In the Gospel of Luke he showed what Jesus *began* to do and to teach so that the reader might have a certainty of those things. Now, in this book Luke is showing what the risen Christ *continues* to do and to teach. This ministry is done by the Holy Spirit through men.

The Book of Acts is a very important book in the New Testament since it shows the beginning of the spread of the gospel to all people and the beginning of the group known as the Church. This book was not written as an explanation of what was happening but to show what was happening. The reader must go to the epistles of the New Testament to see the *why* of the things in this book. Many of the epistles were written during the period covered by this book, and it will be profitable to read them in connection with the events.

Acts was written about A.D. 63. This may be deduced from chapter 28. Paul is in Rome under house arrest. It seems evident from the events in 1 Timothy, 2 Timothy, and Titus that Paul was released from this arrest at the end of two years and that he traveled until he was again arrested and put to death about A.D. 66. Since the Book of Acts does not mention these things, it seems best to date the book where it ends, A.D. 63. With this in mind, it then becomes apparent that the events described in this book cover about thirty years. This book, then, becomes the record of what the Church did to evangelize the world in the first generation.

It should be noted that just as the Gospels do not pretend

to give a complete history of Jesus, this book does not pretend to give a complete history of the time, the events, or the men. A comparison of 2 Corinthians 11–12, Galatians 1–2, and 1 Peter 5 will show events in Paul's life, as well as in Peter's life, that are not found in this book.

This is a book of transitions. The Judaism of the Old Testament is changed to the Christianity of the New. The rule of life for man in most of the Old Testament was the Law, but in the Book of Acts it is clear that the Law is no longer the rule for man. The Law is replaced by the rule of grace or the Spirit. In the Gospels, the disciples had learned to trust in the present Christ. In Acts, they are taught to rely on the risen Christ through the Holy Spirit. The Gospels centered in the Jewish nation and the disciples were first active only in Israel (Matthew 10); but in this book the area is enlarged to include all people.

The important men of Acts include Peter, Stephen, Philip, James, Barnabas, and Paul. The key verse of this book is 1:8, wherein Christ tells the disciples that they are to be witnesses in Jerusalem, Judea, and Samaria, and then to the uttermost part of the earth. This is a geographical division and the book follows this plan. In chapters 1–7, the activity centers in Jerusalem. Then, in Acts 8:1, Luke records that the believers were scattered throughout the regions of Judea and Samaria. In the next few chapters, the witnessing is in these larger sections. In chapter 13, Paul and Barnabas start on the first missionary journey which begins the last section of the book as the gospel is taken to places outside of Palestine.

Since the book uses geographcial references, it is of the utmost importance that the reader be able to follow the book this way. Not only the land of Palestine needs to be known, but the travels of Paul on his journeys are also important. The maps on pages 157–158 will be helpful in this area.

Outline of the Book of Acts

    I   Witness to Jerusalem   1–7
          A   The power for witnessing   1

B The day of Pentecost 2
C The establishing of the church 3–5
D The first martyr 6–7

II Witness in Judea and Samaria 8–12
A Scattering the believers 8
B Conversion of Paul 9
C Preaching of Peter 10–11:18
D Church at Antioch 11:19–30
E Death of James and Herod 12

III Witness to the uttermost 13–28
A First missionary journey 13–14
B First official council 15:1–22
C Second missionary journey 15:28–18:22
D Third missionary journey 18:23–21:17
E Paul in Jerusalem 21:18–26:32
F Paul in Rome 27–28

8
Paul's Epistles

ROMANS

The Book of Romans is considered the foundation of Christian theology. This book relates the work of God to man in a most dynamic fashion. In order to properly understand what Jesus did for man, it is necessary to know this book.

Paul wrote this book while he was in Corinth (compare Romans 16:23 and 1 Corinthians 1:14), near the end of his third journey, as he was about to go to Jerusalem (see Acts 21:1–5 and Romans 15). Paul wrote this epistle for two reasons. First, he wanted to share with the believers at Rome his understanding of the gospel; second he wanted to prepare them for the visit that he planned to make in the near future.

Since the Gospel centers in God's righteousness, the Book of Romans has this great truth as its central thought. The key verses of the book are 1:16–17. Paul is going to show how God has brought about His plan to make man righteous.

The apostle Paul was well trained. He had been schooled to think with the best thinkers (see Acts 17) or he could talk with any person on the street. As a good thinker, he develops this book in a logical manner. The text moves from one great point to another with each section building on the preceding one. First (1–3), he shows that man has a need for the righteousness of God. He then presents how this righteousness is made available to man (3:21–4:25). In the next section (5–8), Paul unfolds what other results are the believer's since he has this righteousness. The fourth section (9–11) is often taken as a parenthesis in the argument of the book since it appears to leave the subject and talk about Israel. It seems better, however, to take this section as a defense of God's righteousness in His dealings with the nation. The final section (12–16) then becomes the application of this righteousness to the everyday life of the believer. Read this book often. Marvel in the work that God has done for man. Share this book with others for this is the gospel.

Outline of the Epistle to the Romans

I   The need for God's righteousness   1–3:20
   A   The Gentile needs it   1:1–32
   B   The Jew needs it   2:1–3:8
   C   All need it   3:9–20

II   The provision of God's righteousness   3:21–4:25
   A   The death of Christ   3:21–26
   B   The avenue of faith   3:27–4:25

III   The results of God's righteousness   5:1–8:39
   A   Possessions in Christ   5:1–21
   B   Freedom in Christ   6:1–7:25
   C   Spirit of Christ   8:1–27
   D   Union with Christ   8:28–29

IV   The defense of God's righteousness   9–11
   A   In Israel's past   9
   B   In Israel's present   10
   C   In Israel's future   11

V   The application of God's righteousness   12–16
   A   Between the believer and God   12:1–8
   B   Between believers   12:9–16
   C   Between believers and unbelievers   12:17–21
   D   Between believers and governments   13:1–7
   E   Between believers and the law of love   13:8–14
   F   Between the believer and his actions   14:1–15:13
   G   Between Paul and the Romans   15:14–33
   H   Between Paul and his friends   16:1–27

1 CORINTHIANS

The Church at Corinth was founded by Paul on his second missionary journey (Acts 18:1–18), during his long stay in this city (Acts 18:11), of at least eighteen months. The city of Corinth was known for its idolatry and immorality, but the gospel is meant for all people.

From the sixteenth chapter it is evident that Paul wrote this letter while he was in Ephesus on his third missionary journey (Acts 19) and just before he left for his trip to Jerusalem. The occasion of this letter is twofold. There were some problems in the church that needed attention (1:11; 5:1) which he wanted to clear up. Also, the people of Corinth had evidently sent a letter to Paul, and he took this opportunity to answer the questions that had been asked (see 7:1; 8:1; 12:1; 16:1).

It is always a dangerous thing when one chapter in the Bible is singled out as very important since this looks as though the other chapters are not important. Truly all Scripture is given by God and is profitable. But the reader is invited to study chapter 15 very carefully. This chapter has a very good explanation of the contents of the gospel and also a very good explanation of the doctrine of resurrection. Every believer should know what this chapter says about these two great subjects.

A very easy way to understand this book is to divide it into the problems Paul wanted to treat (1–6) and the problems the people wanted him to treat (7–16). This is perhaps the best way to go through the book, but an alternative is given so the reader may see a slight variation in approach.

Outline of the Epistle to the Corinthians

    I   Division in the church   1:1–4:21
        A   Men and divisions   1:1–17
        B   Wisdom and division   1:18–3:4
        C   Judgment and divisions   3:5–23
        D   The apostle and division   4:1–21

II Discipline and the church 5–6
  A Regarding immorality 5
  B Regarding civil affairs 6:1–8
  C Regarding social affairs 6:9–20

III Difficulties in the church 7:1–14:40
  A Marriage 7
  B Things sacrificed to idols 8–10
  C The Lord's Supper 11
  D Spiritual gifts 12–14

IV Doctrine in the church 15–16
  A The Gospel 15:1–11
  B The resurrection 15:12–58
  C The offering 16:1–24

2 CORINTHIANS

The Book of 2 Corinthians is the most personal and the most emotional of Paul's books. This makes it very difficult to outline and to organize the material in logical fashion. In order to better understand the connection between 1 and 2 Corinthians and to better understand why it is not an orderly book like the other ones written by Paul, it is necessary to understand some of Paul's movements at this time.

1 Paul visited Corinth on his second journey (Acts 18)
2 Paul stayed at Ephesus for three years on the third journey (Acts 19)
3 There must have been a visit to Corinth during this time (2 Corinthians 12:14 calls the coming visit the third one)
4 This visit was probably a painful one (2 Corinthians 2:1)
5 News came to Paul later about the church
6 Paul wrote 1 Corinthians
7 Paul went to Troas and waited for word from Titus (2 Corinthians 2:12–13)

8 News comes from Corinth that is both good and bad (2 Corinthians 7:6–13; 12:11–21)
9 Paul writes 2 Corinthians out of a heart that is sensitive to these believers (compare 1 Corinthians 4:14; 10:14; 15:58; 2 Corinthians 7:1; 12:19)

When it is said that this book is not orderly, it is not meant that the book lacks order. There are a number of sections in the book and each one of these is orderly. But the development of the book does not flow as do the other books of Paul. Paul was writing as his heart prompted him to write and as the thoughts came to his mind. (This does not take away from the inspiration of the book. The Spirit was still at work to have Paul write what God wanted written.)

The reader is invited to study some of the sections in this book very carefully for they give some of the best information of the subject covered. For an understanding of judgment for the Christian, chapter 5 is a must. Giving is the subject in chapters 8 and 9. The apostles' heart motives and life summary are found in chapters 10 through 12. For a good understanding of the work and person of Satan, the following passages may be noted: 2:11; 4:4; 11:3; 14; 12:7.

It seems easier to follow general chapter divisions in this book rather than an outline.

Divisions of the Second Epistle to the Corinthians

1 The confidence of Paul 1
2 The admonition of Paul 2
3 The ministration of righteousness 3
4 The ministry 4
5 The judgment seat of Christ 5
6 The life of separation 6
7 The heart of Paul 7
8 Giving 8–9
9 Paul's history 10–12
10 Paul's purpose 13

125

GALATIANS

It is normally taken that Paul wrote the Epistle to the Galatians on his third missionary journey, either from Ephesus or from Corinth. This cannot be proven from the book itself since no location or time is given by which a date might be fixed. Many readers of the Bible take the experience in chapter 2, Paul's visit to Jerusalem, to be the visit mentioned in Acts 15, and this would make the epistle after this event. A date of the third missionary journey is usually given to allow time for the Judaizers (those who tried to make Christianity a mixture of the Law and Christ) to make their presence felt. There is a possibility, however, that the epistle could be earlier since the opponents of Christianity were present wherever Paul went. But certainly no problem can be encountered by using the traditional date of late on the third journey.

The occasion of the epistle is indeed an important one. This epistle was written to show that the believer is justified (declared righteous before God) by faith alone without the works of the Law or any legal system, and to show that the believer is also kept by this same faith and not by works that might be done. Both of these aspects are seen in 1:4, and the two ideas are carried throughout the book (compare 2:21; 3:3; 5:5).

Romans and Galatians should be studied together. Romans shows the need and basis of a man finding God's righteousness, and Galatians shows that the manner of obtaining this righteousness is by faith and not by any connection with the Law or legal activities. Christianity needs to keep these two books always in the foreground to prevent error from coming into the presentation of the Gospel. Lest one should think that this is not important, Paul's words in Galatians 1:6–9 should be read and memorized.

The Book of Galatians is an easy one to think through. The book is made up of six chapters, and there are three divisions of two chapters each. In order to combat the Judaizers, Paul first shows that his apostleship came straight from the risen

Lord; he is, therefore, giving the true message. After showing that he is a true messenger of God, he then declares the message that God would have him preach. As a final help to the Galatians, he shows how the life of faith is to be lived in contrast to what the Judaizers would say.

Outline of the Epistle to the Galatians

I   Vindication of Paul's Gospel   1–2   (Personal)
   A   Paul's message is from God   1:1–24
   B   Paul's mission is from God   2:1–10
   C   Paul's manner is from God   2:11–21

II   Explanation of Paul's Gospel   3–4   (Doctrinal)
   A   Taught by example   3:1–14
   B   Taught by contrast   3:15–22
   C   Taught by analogy   3:23–4:7
   D   Taught by desire   4:8–20
   E   Taught by allegory   4:21–31

III   Application of Paul's Gospel   5–6   (Practical)
   A   Life of freedom stated   5:1
   B   Hinderance to freedom rebuked   5:2–12
   C   Use of freedom outlined   5:13–15
   D   Combat of freedom described   5:16–24
   E   Life of freedom explained   5:25–6:18

EPHESIANS

With the Epistle to the Ephesians, the reader of the Bible is brought to the first of what is often called the "Prison Epistles." These epistles are Ephesians, Philippians, Colossians, and Philemon. They are called by this name since all four were written from Rome during Paul's first imprisonment. In these four letters Paul writes one to an individual (Philemon), two to local churches (Colossians and Philippians), and one to the churches in general (Ephesians). All four show what it means to be "in Christ" and how important it is to live in proper relation to the risen Saviour.

Ephesians is usually taken as being intended for the churches in general rather than a local church in particular. Two main reasons for this are: (1) in some of the ancient manuscripts the words "at Ephesus" are missing, thus showing the letter was intended for all saints; and (2) there are no local references in this epistle as normally found in other epistles addressed to one local group.

In reading through the New Testament in the order found in the English Bible, it is almost like coming out of the storm into a calm when this book is reached. After the controversies and problems of 1 and 2 Corinthians and Galatians, Ephesians is indeed a peaceable book; there is no controversy in this epistle. It was written to show the believer's relation to all that Christ has done.

Paul is certainly the master of figures of speech when it comes to the writers of the epistles. In this book the believer is spoken of in terms relating to a body (1), a temple (2), a mystery (3), a new man (4), a bride (5), and a soldier (6). Each of these are worthy of considerable mention by every reader of the Bible.

This epistle is typical of Paul's style. In the first section or sections of a letter, Paul describes what God has done for the believer. In the last section Paul describes how the believer is to conduct himself in the light of the truths just mentioned. These six chapters divide evenly in this respect. Chapters 1–3 relate the believer to the heavenly scene and chapters 4–6 relate the believer to the earthly scene.

Outline of the Epistle to the Ephesians

I The believer's position in Christ in the heavenlies 1–3
   A Within the work of the Trinity 1:1–14
   B Raised and seated with Christ 1:15–2:10
   C Joined together with God 2:11–22
   D Made part of the mystery 3:1–21

II The believer's position in Christ in this world 4–6
   A Our walk in unity 4:1–16
   B Our walk in separation 4:17–29

C   Our walk in God   4:30–5:20
D   Our walk in society   5:21–6:9
E   Our walk in combat   6:10–24

PHILIPPIANS

The Epistle to the Philippians could be called a letter of joy. One might think that Paul would have bitter memories of his experiences in the city of Philippi because of his imprisonment and beating, but just the opposite is true. Just as Paul was found praising God in the jail at midnight (Acts 16:25), so he is found praising God at every remembrance of this group of believers.

From the house where Paul was under arrest (Acts 28:30) and in bondage to Roman guards (Philippians 1:7, 13) came this letter to the Philippians. Epaphroditus had come from Philippi with a gift for Paul (4:18) and then had become sick (2:25–30). When he had recovered sufficiently, Paul must have sent him back with this letter to cheer the hearts of the church at Philippi.

The key to this epistle is to see that Christ is the source of all the believer's joy. No matter what the circumstances may be, it is always possible to rejoice in Christ. As this epistle is read, note the repetition of the idea of *being in Christ*. This is worth seeing. Two key verses in this epistle are 1:21 and 3:1.

Outline of the Epistle to the Philippians

I   The basis of our life   1
  A   Prayer for the Philippians   1:1–11
  B   Experiences of Paul   1:12–19
  C   Expectation of Paul   1:20–30

II   Motivation for the life   2
  A   Christ the example   2:1–11
  B   Christians the lights   2:12–16
  C   Timothy and Epaphroditus   2:17–30

129

III   The object of the life   3
    A   To know Christ   3:1–11
    B   To look toward Christ   3:12–19
    C   To look for Christ   3:20–21

IV   The secret of the life   4
    A   Labor with Christ   4:1–4
    B   Live with Christ   4:5–7
    C   Think with Christ   4:8–9
    D   Learn with Christ   4:10–12
    E   Lean on Christ   4:13–23

COLOSSIANS

The key to the Epistle to the Colossians is clearly stated in 1:18, "that in all things He [Christ] might mave the pre-eminence." Paul wants all to know that the only thing that counts is the position of Christ in one's life. This is the key to all Christian living and to real Christianity.

The church at Colosse may have been founded by a fellow worker of Paul rather than by Paul himself. In 1:7, Paul refers to learning of the Gospel from Epaphras, and in 2:1, he implies that the believers in Colosse had not seen his face. It is possible that this church came into being during Paul's stay at Ephesus when he promoted the spread of the Gospel throughout all of Asia Minor (Acts 19:10).

The Epistle of Colossians and the Epistle of Philemon go together in the sense that they both are addressed to people in the same location. In fact, it can be seen that Onesimus carried the letter to Philemon while Tychicus carried the letter to the church (4:7–9).

From the contents of this book it seems that Paul was trying to handle two problems in writing this letter. The believers at Colosse were evidently losing sight of the supreme headship of Christ in their every affair. Also, a form of gnosticism was creeping into the church, and this error needed to be handled. Gnosticism was a heresy of the first century which taught that

God did not create the world, but that some semigod did; that Jesus really was a semigod and not God Himself; that special knowledge was available to understand the great things of God; and that asceticism was a virtue. These heresies are dealt with in this book.

The Book of Colossians and the Book of Ephesians are very similar in content. Many of the things written in Ephesians are also in this book with a slight change of wording. Compare the prayer of Colossians 1 with the prayer of Ephesians 1; the mystery of Colossians 1:24–29 with Ephesians 3; and the section Colossians 3:5–4:6 with Ephesians 5:21–6:9. The general twofold division of Ephesians is also seen in Colossians in that doctrine is iterated first then practice is discussed.

Outline of the Epistle to the Colossians

    I   Christology   1:1–2:19
          A   In the prayer of Paul   1:1–23
          B   In the ministry of Paul   1:24–2:5
          C   In the doctrine of Paul   2:6–19

    II   Christianity   2:20–4:18
          A   The character of Christianity   2:20–3:4
          B   Christianity and society   3:5–17
          C   Christianity and the family   3:18–21
          D   Christianity and labor   3:22–4:1
          E   Christianity and speech   4:2–6
          F   Christianity and friends   4:7–18

1 THESSALONIANS

The Epistle of Paul to the Thessalonians was the first one he wrote. Among other things, this lets it be known what the apostle did early in his ministry and what the early church was taught.

The founding of the church at Thessalonica is recorded in Acts 17. Paul came from Philippi to Thessalonica and spent three sabbaths in the local synagogue reasoning with the Jews. The narration is not clear as to how much longer he stayed in the city. It is possible that this church was founded and instructed in just four short weeks. Even though he might have stayed a longer time, it is certain that his stay in this city was a relatively short one.

The occasion and time of the writing of this letter are given in chapter 3 of the letter. Paul relates how he went to Athens and stayed there alone while Timothy was sent back to Thessalonica to see how things were going (compare Acts 17). Timothy and Silas returned to Paul when he was in Corinth (Acts 18:5), and this return brought cheer to the apostle (1 Thessalonians 3:6). It was this delight in the people plus a question concerning the return of Christ, as discussed in chapters 4 and 5, that caused Paul to pen this letter. This epistle was written, therefore, during his stay in Corinth on the second journey.

Since this is an early epistle of Paul, it is interesting to note the truths taught or referred to in it. It is clear that Paul taught all the major truths to this church even though his stay there was short. As this book unfolds, the following subjects are seen: the deity of Christ (called "Lord" some forty times), His vicarious death, His physical resurrection, the conversion of the sinner, a holy walk, the Lord's return, and many other essentials of Christianity. This epistle shows that Christian theology did not evolve; rather, it was the product of the revelation of God.

Certainly one of the keys to this book is the truth of the return of Jesus. This fact is mentioned in every chapter of the book (1:10; 2:19; 3:13; 4:15–16; 5:23). The early church had this fact of the return of the Lord as a central thought in their life.

This letter can be divided into two sections each ending in a prayer. Chapters 1 through 3 form the first division, and the subject matter is in the personal realm. The last two chapters are the second unit, and the subject matter is in the realm of practical truths for the Thessalonians' lives.

I   Personal matters   1–3
   A   Praise for the Thessalonians   1
   B   Practice of the evangelists   2:1–12
   C   Problems of the Thessalonians   2:13–16
   D   Passion of the apostle   2:17–3:10
   E   Prayer for the Thessalonians   3:11–13

II   Practical matters   4–5:28
   A   Concerning the walk of the believer   4:1–12
   B   Concerning the waiting of the believer   4:13–18
   C   Concerning the work of the believer   5:1–11
   D   Concerning the will of God for the believer
       5:12–22
   E   Prayer for the Thessalonians   5:23–28

2 THESSALONIANS

The conditions leading to the writing of this second letter to the church at Thessalonica are essentially the same as the first. The two letters were written very close together. The reason this second one had to be written so soon is twofold. Some believers were looking so earnestly for the return of Christ that they had stopped all meaningful activity, and this needed to be corrected. There was also a false teaching that had started evidently by someone forging a letter from Paul (2:2), saying that the believers were then going through the time of trouble that was coming upon the earth. Paul shows in this epistle that the believer is to "work while waiting" and that God will deliver the believer from the earth before the trouble starts.

It was true that the believers at Thessalonica were experiencing troubles. This was how they began their Christian experience, and it was continuing. What this letter does is to encourage the suffering saint by showing that this suffering is temporal and light compared to the future suffering God has prepared for the unbeliever.

The book can be understood by seeing Paul's answer to three problems.

Problems in the Second Epistle to the Thessalonians

1   The problem of persecutions is handled by telling them to rest in God   1
2   The problem of prophecy is handled by telling them to understand God's program   2
3   The problem of their practice is handled by telling them that work is essential for living   3

1 TIMOTHY

First Timothy is one of the three epistles known as the Pastoral Epistles, so designated because they were written to pastors to help them with the care of the churches. The other two in this group are 2 Timothy and Titus. The two books that bear Timothy's name were written to this "young man" while he was in charge of the churches in Ephesus. The Book of Titus was written to Titus while he was ministering on the isle of Crete.

Paul wrote these three books after the period covered by the Book of Acts. When Acts ended, Paul was in Rome under house arrest awaiting his trial with the Jews from Jerusalem as his accusers. It is evident that they never showed up and that Paul was released. It is during this time of future travels not covered by Acts that Paul left Timothy at Ephesus and Titus at Crete. When we come to 2 Timothy, Paul is again in Rome and in prison with the sentence of death hanging over his head.

The theme in 1 Timothy is the pattern of a good minister and a good church. This book shows how a group of believers should organize and function. The pattern is not in detail, but there is enough given to show every church that wants to know about God's work how it is proper to act.

Outline of the First Epistle to Timothy

I   Paul's charge to a young church   1:1–3:16
   A   Purity in doctrine   1:1–20
   B   Purity in actions   2:1–15
   C   Purity in officers   3:1–16

II Paul's charge to a young pastor   4:1–6:21
   A   His relation to good doctrine   4:1–16
   B   His relation to the church   5:1–6:2
   C   His relation to himself   6:3–21

2 TIMOTHY

The Book of 2 Timothy is Paul's last letter of record. Soon after this letter was written, Paul was beheaded as a prisoner of Rome. This then becomes the last will and testament of the great apostle who spread the Gospel over the then known world.

That the events in 2 Timothy cannot be the events of Acts 28 is evident because: (1) during his two-year stay he was confident of his release (Philippians 2:23–24; Philemon 22) while in this book he is confident he will die; (2) according to 2 Timothy 4:20 he left Trophimus sick at Miletum and this does not fit Acts 20:4, 17; and 20:29, when Paul was on his way to Jerusalem, nor does it fit his trip to Rome since he did not pass that way (Acts 27–28); and (3) in 1 Timothy 1:3, Paul had left Timothy in Ephesus and this also cannot be found in Acts. Paul must have been released, again traveled during which these events took place, and then must have been arrested again. This brings us to the Book of 2 Timothy.

First Timothy had to do more with the church and the relation of the minister to it, while 2 Timothy has more to do with the minister and the combating of false doctrines that will arise. The only answer to these areas is a continuation in and a study of the Word of God. One of the key words in both of these epistles is the word "doctrine." This word is just another word for the "teachings" of the Bible. Any and every man of God needs to be settled in the Word of God.

Outline of the Second Epistle to Timothy

I   Praise for the past   1:1–18
   A   Godly heritage   1:1–5
   B   Gift of God   1:6–7
   C   God's faithfulness   1:8–14
   D   Godly contrast   1:15–18

II   Patterns for the present   2:1–26
   A   Teaching   2:1–2
   B   Soldier   2:3–4
   C   Trackman   2:5
   D   Husbandman   2:6
   E   General principles   2:7–13
   F   Workman   2:14–15
   G   General precautions   2:16–19
   H   Vessels   2:20–23
   I   Servant   2:24–26

III   Precautions for the future   3:1–4:5
   A   Character of the Times   3:1–9
   B   Contrast of Paul   3:10–12
   C   Doctrine   3:13–14
   D   Scriptures   3:15–17
   E   Preaching   4:1–5

IV   Personal matters   4:6–22
   A   Personal testimony   4:6–8
   B   Personal desires   4:9–18
   C   Personal salutation   4:19–22

TITUS

Titus was a sometime companion of Paul. He is not mentioned as often as Timothy is, and not a great deal is known of him. Paul tells us that Titus was somewhat of a test case of a Gentile keeping the Law (Galatians 2:3–5); further, he worked with Paul in Ephesus and was a letter carrier to the Corinthians (2 Corinthians 2:13; 7:6; 12:18).

The Book of Titus is interesting in that the word "work" appears in every chapter, and this is the central idea of the letter. Paul was the apostle of grace in terms of the condition for salvation and in terms of the believer's life, but this did not mean a life of inactivity or a life of ease. The believer is required to be zealous of (2:14), to be ready to (3:1), to be ready to maintain (3:8), and to learn to maintain (3:14) good works. But lest someone get the wrong idea, Paul is quick to add that salvation does not come because of any good work, but by grace through faith (3:5–8).

It is possible to use 2:12 as the key verse for this epistle and to divide the contents according to the three words "soberly, righteously, and godly." Paul wants this pastor to know the manner of life that needs to be lived in this world as a good representative of Christ.

Outline of the Epistle to Titus

   I Living righteously in the church   1:1–16
      A   Characteristics of true leaders   1:1–9
      B   Characteristics of false leaders   1:10–12
      C   Characteristics of unbelievers   1:13–16

  II Living soberly in the home   2:1–15
      A   Family relations   2:1–6
      B   Titus' example   2:7–8
      C   Domestic relations   2:9–10
      D   Basic philosophy   2:11–15

 III Living godly in the world   3:1–15
      A   Proper life   3:1–3
      B   Personal salvation   3:4–7
      C   Profitable maintenance   3:8–16

PHILEMON

The fourth Prison Epistle of Paul is the short letter addressed to Philemon and was written at the same time as the letter to the Colossians (compare Colossians 4:7–9, 17 and Philemon 2, 10, 23, 24). In the four Prison Epistles it is possible to see Paul as the theologian (Ephesians), as the saint (Philippians), as the apologist (Colossians), and as the gentleman (Philemon).

The occasion of this letter is simple. Philemon had a servant named Onesimus who had wronged him and had run away. This put the death sentence automatically upon the head of this slave. Onesimus fled from Colosse to Rome, and there he came in contact with Paul who led him to believe in Christ. Now Paul is sending Onesimus back to Philemon, and he is writing this letter of request for the runaway slave. This is a beautiful example of a Christian gentleman at work.

This small letter is also a beautiful example of what Christ has done for the believer. Onesimus had the death sentence over his head and he needed someone to plead his cause for him. This person had to know both Philemon and Onesimus. Further, the only way Onesimus could be justly restored would be for the debt to be paid. All of this Paul did and more. Paul knew Onesimus; he knew Philemon; he was willing to pay any debt Onesimus had; and Paul was willing to have all his own credit transferred to this slave. This is the gospel story of the real substitution made by Christ for the sinner. We needed someone to plead our cause with God, and this one had to be equal with God and with us. This One is Jesus. To be just, we needed someone to pay our debt, and this Jesus did when He died on the cross. Further, we need to have God's righteousness to enter heaven, and this is provided by Christ for us. Thus, this simple story of the Book of Philemon is a good way to tell the story of redemption in everyday language.

Outline of the Epistle to Philemon

    I   Paul's greeting   1–3
   II   Paul's praise   4–7
  III   Paul's request   8–20
  IV   Paul's confidence   21–22
   V   Paul's benediction   23–25

HEBREWS

The Book of Hebrews is the book of the New Testament about which there is the most discussion of its authorship. No name of an author appears in the book, and not much is given to establish authorship. Many claim that Paul could not have written the book since the style and the vocabulary are not his; nor does the book contain his name; further, he was the apostle to the Gentiles. Others claim Paul was the writer because his benediction appears (13:22–25), because Timothy is named, and because Paul had a great concern for Israel. Also, 2 Peter 3:15–16 implies Paul wrote to the Jews.

Although the authorship cannot be firmly established, the theme of the book can be established. It was written to show how great Christ is and how much better He is than Judaism or anything or any person. The word *perfection* is used eleven times (2:10; 5:9; 6:1; 7:11, 19; 9:9; 10:1, 14; 11:40; 12:23; 13:21) and the words *better than* occur thirteen times (1:4; 6:9; 7:7, 19, 22; 8:6 twice; 9:23; 10:34; 11:16, 35, 40; 12:24). The writer is proving that Jesus is the answer to all God has for man.

An important feature of this book is that it shows the work Jesus is doing in heaven for the believer while we await His return. Romans shows what Jesus did on the cross for the believer. The Books of Paul to the Thessalonians keep our eyes open for the future coming of Christ (which could be at any time). Then Hebrews lets us rejoice in the present work of Christ.

Hebrews can be grasped by seeing the movement of the writer in three areas. Christ is proven to be better in His person, in His performance, and in His provision. The first two sections are related to a comparison with Judaism, and the last section is just a statement of what Christ provides without too much contrast or comparison.

Outline of the Epistle to the Hebrews

I   Christ is better in His person   1–7
   A   Because He is God   1:1–3

B   Compared to angels   1:4–2:18
C   Compared to Moses   3:1–19
D   Compared to Joshua   4:1–13
E   Compared to Abraham   4:14–7:7
F   Compared to Levi   7:8–28

II   Christ is better in His performance   8:1–10:18
   A   Based on a better covenant   8:1–13
   B   Based on a heavenly sanctuary   9:1–11
   C   Based on His own blood   9:12–28
   D   Based on a finished work   10:1–18

III   Christ is better in His provision   10:19–13:25
   A   Full assurance   10:19–39
   B   Faith life   11:1–40
   C   Complete training   12:1–11
   D   Perfect possession   12:12–29
   E   Full instructions   13:1–25

9

General Epistles
and the Revelation

JAMES

With the Book of James, we are brought to a group of books in the New Testament known as the General or Catholic Epistles since they are not addressed to a local group or person. This set includes James, 1 and 2 Peter, 1, 2, and 3 John, and Jude. The short letters of 2 and 3 John are included in this group even though they are addressed to individuals.

The author of the Book of James was one of the brothers (half-brothers, since they had the same mother but not the same father) of Jesus. He is named along with his brothers in Matthew 13:55 and Mark 6:3. This James should not be confused with the James who was the brother of John or with James the son of Alphaeus, who was also a disciple (Matthew 10:2–3). This James was not a believer in Jesus until after the resurrection (compare John 7:5, 10; 1 Corinthians 15:7; and Acts 1:14). He became the leader of the church at Jerusalem and presided at the council, as recorded in Acts 15.

The epistle is taken as the first of the writings of the New Testament, and it shows the life of the church at this early date (before A.D. 50). The book is addressed to Jews that were scattered around the Mediterranean Sea who were believers in Christ also.

The purpose of this book is to show how *the faith* is to be lived. James is not showing works in contrast to faith; rather he

141

is showing that real faith produces certain things in the life. These things can then be used as tests to see if the reader is experiencing and enjoying real faith or if he is just experiencing a belief in some creed.

The tests or proofs of one's faith are seen in four general realms. First, James brings the individual in view; then he presents the individual in relation to others. In the third section James holds up certain things or features in the life as a guide; and finally he asks us to check our philosophy of life.

Outline of the General Epistle of James

I The proof of faith in regard to self   1:1–27
   A Testings   1:1–8
   B Positions   1:9–11
   C Temptations   1:12–18
   D Actions   1:19–27

II The proof of faith in regard to others   2:1–26
   A Not to be with respect of persons   2:1–13
   B Not to be without works   2:14–26

III The proof of faith in regard to things   3:1–4:17
   A To the tongue   3:1–12
   B To true wisdom   3:13–18
   C To the world   4:1–10
   D To judging   4:11–12
   E To the will of God   4:13–17

IV The proof of faith in regard to our
                            philosophy of life   5:1–20
   A Fruitful   5:1–11
   B Truthful   5:12
   C Prayerful   5:13–18
   D Helpful   5:19–20

1 PETER

It is fitting that Peter was allowed to write some of the Bible. This man, for all his blunders as recorded in the Gospels, was indeed a pillar of the church and of the truth after Pentecost. Much has been written about Peter's actions, but unfortunately little is known about what he wrote.

It is not certain when or from where Peter wrote this letter to the Jews. The date for the epistle is usually given as sometime in the 60's before Paul's death. This is usually accepted since the believers are seen as suffering severe persecutions. The place of writing is stated to be Babylon (5:13), but it is not certain whether Peter was speaking of the literal city on the Euphrates where there was a colony of Jews or whether he was using the term to speak of another city which could be characterized by this word. The other city suggested is Rome since it was the political capital of that portion of the world where Christians suffered persecution.

Jesus Christ is central in this book. In chapter 1 He is seen as the Lamb of God; in chapter 2 He is pictured as the chief cornerstone and the one who died for the sins of the world; in chapter 3 He is again seen as dying for the world and as an example of suffering; and finally, in chapter 5 He is seen as coming to reward His servants. The churches and believers of today could learn a great deal from this leader in the early church. Christ must be central in the life of the church and in the life of the believer.

The Book of 1 Peter is really a great piece of literature in the sense of development. Peter is often pictured as ignorant, but his book does not show that fact. Peter has very smoothly shown what the Christian is "called to" in this book by showing the four major aspects of the Christian life. The Christian life must begin with salvation; this is his first section. The main calling of a believer is then to be pure in his life; this is the second section. One of the chief characteristics of a Christian is submission, which is explained in the third division. The book concludes with the idea that in this life there will be suffering.

Outline of the First Epistle General of Peter

I   Salvation   1:1–12
    A   Heaven based   1:1–5

    B   Joy producting   1:6–9

    C   Prophet searched   1:10–12

II   Sanctification   1:13–2:12

    A   On the basis of the person of God   1:13–17

    B   On the basis of the preciousness of Christ's blood   1:18–22

    C   On the basis of the purity of the Word   1:23–2:4

    D   On the basis of our position in God   2:5–12

III   Subjection   2:13–3:12

    A   Principle established   2:13–20

    B   Principle illustrated   2:21–25

    C   Principle applied   3:1–12

IV   Suffering   3:13–5:14

    A   Strength in suffering   3:13–4:1

    B   Source of suffering   4:2–6

    C   Faithfulness in suffering   4:7–13

    D   Cause for suffering   4:14–19

    E   Course in suffering   5:1–14

2 PETER

This short letter was probably written very near the time of Peter's death (1:14), and it may have been written after the death of Paul. This would make this book similar to 2 Timothy in point of time in the writer's life. It is also interesting that the two books are similar in content. Both show the writer knew his death was near; both show a great confidence in their appearing before God; both speak of the false teaching to invade the church; and both show that the answer to the problem is the Word of God.

Key words in this epistle are the word *knowledge* and related words. Peter is convinced that the believer needs to have facts in his mind concerning certain things if he also is to be ready to live a life that can show confidence at the appearing of Christ.

This book is brief enough to take the major paragraphs as divisions and to think through the contents in a progressive manner.

Outline of the Second Epistle General of Peter

1:1–11	The believer is encouraged to develop his spiritual life by—
1:12–21	The Word of God, which is a sure foundation.
2:1–22	False teachers are coming who will not follow sound teaching, such as—
3:1–7	The coming of the Lord, and since He is coming—
3:8–13	We should have our lives pure and—
3:14–18	Grow in the knowledge of Christ.

1 JOHN

The apostle John outlived the other apostles. He had a long and fruitful life and was allowed to write not only a gospel, telling of Christ's life on earth, but the Book of Revelation, telling of the coming again of Jesus. The space in the believer's life between his understanding of the work of Christ on his behalf and the time that Jesus calls for him either through death or through His coming is to be lived in a proper relationship to these two events. It is this life in the Son that John writes about in his epistles.

John shows that the sin question has been settled and provided for in the death of Jesus as the substitute for man (1:9–2:2). Eternal life is now available for any and every man who will believe in this work (5:1–13), and the manner of life after accepting this gift is to be such as to render the believer comfortable in the presence of Christ when He returns (2:28).

The Book of 1 John is unlocked by two keys. The one is found in 1:3–4, where enjoyment of the fellowship of the believer with God and with fellow believers is stated as the purpose of writing. The second is recorded in 5:13, where John states that assurance of eternal life is the purpose of writing. Taking these two keys, it is seen, therefore, that John wants the believer to know he has eternal life since he has believed in the Son and to enjoy all that there is for him in this life.

Outline of the First Epistle General of John

I   Maintenance of fellowship   1:1–2:29
    A   The person involved   1:1–4
    B   The issue involved   1:5–7
    C   The obstacle removed   1:8–2:2
    D   The condition continues   2:3–29

II   Manifestation of fellowship   3:1–4:21
    A   Doing righteously   3:1–10
    B   Loving the brethren   3:11–24
    C   Discerning the spirits   4:1–6
    D   Loving one another   4:7–21
                           (repeated for emphasis)

III   Privileges of fellowship   5:1–21
    A   Overcoming the world   5:1–12
    B   Assurance of eternal life   5:13
    C   Answered prayers   5:14–17
    D   Victory over sin   5:18–19
    E   Understanding of Christ   5:20–21

2 AND 3 JOHN

The Books of 2 and 3 John can be taken together, not only because they are so short, but because they have the same central idea. The key word in these two epistles is *truth,* and the key phrase is *walking in the truth* (2 John 4, 6; 3 John 3).

Second John can be easily remembered as a letter to a lady about her children who were walking in the truth. These children are contrasted with deceivers who are in the world that do not walk either in this manner or with the proper doctrine.

Third John is easy to remember since it is built around statements concerning three men. Two of these men are examples of walking in the truth while the third is an example of walking in the flesh.

Outline of the Second Epistle General of John

    I   Salutation   1–3
   II   Condemnation   4–6
 III   Exhortation   7–11
 IV   Benediction   12–13

Outline of the Third Epistle General of John

   I   Gaius   1–8
  II   Diotrephes   9–11
 III   Demetrius   12–14

JUDE

Jude was another of the half-brothers of Jesus (Matthew 13:55), and he calls himself the brother of James, which relates him to the author of the Book of James. It is obvious that Jude is using James' name since he was the leader of the church, and this would give him a hearing or at least clearly identify who this Jude was. It is revealing that neither James nor Jude made any claim to being a physical relation of Jesus. They took their place at the foot of the cross and became brothers to all believers rather than use their family association based on their mother Mary.

The date of the book is difficult to establish. The only clue is the similarity of this book to the Book of 2 Peter. Most readers of the Bible date these two books about the same time, that is, the last part of the 60s.

Jude is very clear in this book as to his purpose. He had wanted to write to the believers to encourage them in the faith, but circumstances made it necessary that he write to them concerning the departure from the faith that some had made and to encourage the believers to contend for the faith (3–4).

Outline of the General Epistle of Jude

I   Salutation   1–4
        (Note the preservation in face of the apostasy)
     A   Greeting   1–2
     B   Purpose   3–4

II Judgment upon apostasy   5–19
     A   History and apostasy   5–7
     B   Description of apostates   8–16
     C   Warning of apostasy   17–19

III Safeguard against apostasy   20–23
     A   Walk in respect to self   20–21
     B   Walk in respect to others   22–23

IV Benediction   24–25
        (Note: God described as protection from apostasy)
     A   His power   24
     B   His person   25

THE REVELATION

The last book of the English Bible is The Revelation of St. John the Divine. This title is not altogether accurate. The real title for the book is found in verse 1. There the title is The Revelation of Jesus Christ. This makes the last book in the Bible focus on Jesus Christ just as the whole Bible has been pointing to Him. It is almost as if the whole Bible is like a giant funnel with its large opening at the top and then narrowing down to a small opening at the bottom. The Bible started out in broad language, speaking of the coming Redeemer and God's plan for the world. By the last book this has been narrowed down to the person of Jesus, His death on the cross, and His return to the earth to rule in the kingdoms of men.

The Book of the Revelation is usually considered a book on prophecy, and so it is; but it can be studied for what it says about Christ, His names, His titles, His attributes, and His works. This book is about Him.

Many Christians will not read this book because they feel they cannot understand it. This is strange since the book is called a *revelation*, not a *hiding*. This lack of reading of The Revelation is also a shame since God has promised a blessing to the reader of it (1:3). This book, like the others in the Bible, is given by God and is profitable.

The problem most people have with this book is how much to read literally and how much to take figuratively. There is no easy answer to this question. The book does use many symbols and speaks in an abundance of figures. A suggested pattern would be to take the things literally unless the rest of the Bible speaks against it or unless the particular context is such as to show that it is meant only as a symbol.

John wrote this book while he was in exile on the isle of Patmos. God gave this great unfolding of the future as it centers in His Son to this man who, like Daniel, was a man greatly loved by Christ (John 13:23). The things in this book are the product of what John was shown and what was told to John while he was taken into the future by a vision from God.

The obvious key to the things written in this book is found in 1:19. John records how he was told to write in three sections or concerning three specific parts of the revelation. First, he is to record the things he has seen—the vision of the risen Christ. Then he is to write the things that pertain to the present situation with the churches. Finally he is to write the things that will be in the future.

Outline of the Book of the Revelation

I The things he has seen 1:1–19
   A Title and blessing 1:1–3
   B Salutation and description 1:4–8
   C Vision and command 1:9–19

II The things which are 1:20–3:22
   A Message to Ephesus 1:20–2:7
   B Message to Smyrna 2:8–11
   C Message to Pergamos 2:12–17
   D Message to Thyatira 2:18–29

E Message to Sardis 3:1–6
F Message to Philadelphia 3:7–13
G Message to Laodicea 3:14–22

III Things which shall be after this 4:1–22:7
A Throne room in heaven 4–5
B The six seals 6
C The two multitudes 7
D The six trumpets 8–9
E The two visions 10:1–11:13
F The seventh trumpet 11:14–19
G The people of the times 12–13
H The words of the angels 14
I The seven vials 15–16
J Babylon 17–18
K The return of Christ 19
L The Kingdom 20:1–10
M The Great White Throne 20:11–15
N The new things 21–22:7

IV The last words 22:8–21
A Words of the angel 22:8–9
B Words of Christ 22:10–20a
C Words of John 22:20b–21

10

Conclusion

The Bible is a beautiful book and one that is full of meaning. A story is being told on its pages, and the meaning of the story can never grow old or obsolete. It has been the aim of this book to make the Bible more understandable by simply showing the story that is being told and how each fits into the picture.

There is no short cut to understanding the Bible. Neither this book nor any other book can take the place of reading the Bible itself. This book is only intended to give the Bible reader a small insight into the direction of the Word of God so that he can feel more at home. If you are not reading the Bible along with these suggestions for direction, you will not be able to understand what the meaning really is.

The key that unlocks all of the Bible is not found in merely understanding the message or story of the book. The only real key is to know personally the One of whom the book speaks. To know Jesus Christ is to have the key to understanding. He told the Jews this very fact, as recorded in John 5:39–40.

The way to know Jesus Christ is simple. The Bible clearly shows that although man was created by God and in a right relation to Him, man disobeyed God, and by that act men became condemned of sin and subject to the complete judgment of God.

Since man cannot work for, earn, or in any way regain that right relation with God by his own efforts, God has taken upon Himself to provide a way. Jesus Christ is that way.

When Jesus died on the cross, He died in the place of every

human being. He took the judgment that was due us and by His death satisfied the justice and holiness of God. Now man is called upon to believe that Jesus did take the sinner's place on the cross and is to receive the living Jesus into his life. Upon doing this man has his sin forgiven and has the righteousness of God rendered to his account as well. This gives man eternal life and guarantees that heaven will be his final home (read Romans 3:23; 6:23; 2 Corinthians 5:21).

It is this act of putting all your confidence in the work of Jesus Christ—completely abandoning all efforts of your own— that brings you into a knowledge of Jesus and gives you the key to understanding. You must receive Jesus as your Saviour to understand. Do not try to understand first and then believe. See your need of a Saviour, see the complete work of Christ on the cross, receive Him as our personal Saviour, and *live to understand.*

May God bless you as you read *His Word!*

Appendixes

Historical Comparisons

Formation	Deliverance	Wanderings	Conquering	Declension	Saul	David	Division	Captivity	Exile	Temple	City	Silent	Christ	Church	Completion
Genesis	Exodus	Numbers	Joshua	Judges	1 Samuel	2 Samuel	1 Kings	2 Kings	Daniel	Ezra	Nehemiah	years	Gospels	Acts	1 Timothy through Revelation
2000 B.C.	1500				1000			722	606	536	400		6 B.C. A.D. 32	A.D. 66	A.D. 100
Abraham	Moses				Saul David Solomon		Assyria		Babylon	End of Old Testament			Birth of Christ Death of Christ	Death of Paul	Death of John

Temple

Genesis	Exodus	Numbers	Joshua	Judges	1 Samuel	2 Samuel	1 Kings	2 Kings	Daniel	Ezra	Nehemiah	Silent	Christ	Church	Completion
Job	Leviticus Deuteronomy			Ruth		Psalms	Song of Solomon Proverbs Ecclessiastes	Note 1	Ezekiel	Esther Haggai Zechariah	Malachi	years	Matthew Mark Luke John	Note 2	Note 3

——— 1 - 2 Chronicles ———

Note 1. Isaiah, Jeremiah, Lamentation, Hosea, Joel, Amos, Obadiah, Jonah, Micah, Nahum, Habakkuk, and Zephaniah.

Note 2. Romans, 1-2 Corinthians, Galatians, Ephesians, Philippians, Colossians, 1-2 Thessalonians, Philemon, Hebrews, James.

Note 3. 1-2 Timothy, Titus, 1-2 Peter, 1-3 John, Jude, Revelation.

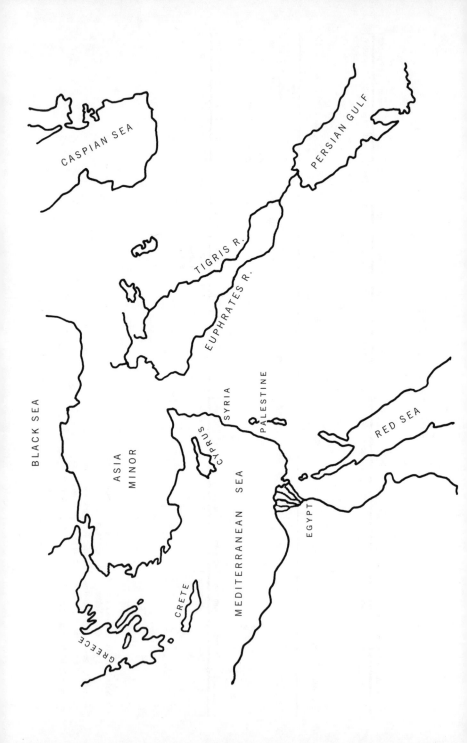

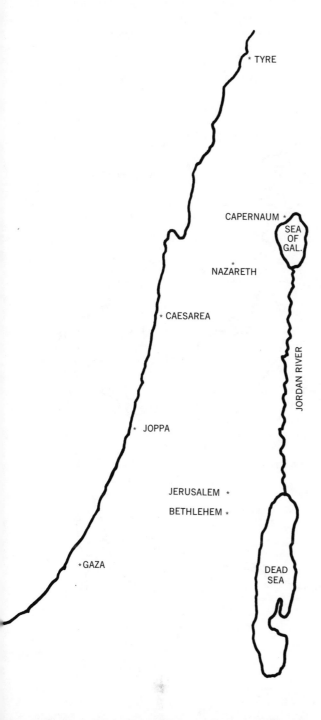

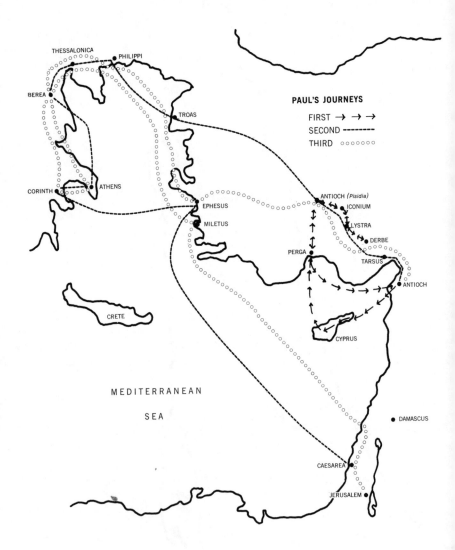

PAUL'S JOURNEYS

FIRST → → →
SECOND -------
THIRD ○○○○○○○

THESSALONICA
PHILIPPI
BEREA
TROAS
CORINTH
ATHENS
EPHESUS
MILETUS
ANTIOCH (Pisidia)
ICONIUM
LYSTRA
DERBE
PERGA
TARSUS
ANTIOCH
CRETE
CYPRUS
MEDITERRANEAN
SEA
DAMASCUS
CAESAREA
JERUSALEM